easy tagine

Delicious recipes for Moroccan one-pot cooking

with recipes by
Ghillie Başan

RYLAND PETERS & SMALL
LONDON • NEW YORK

Senior Designer Toni Kay
Editor Ellen Parnavelas
Picture Research Christina Borsi
Production Laura Grundy
Art Director Leslie Harrington
Editorial Director Julia Charles

Indexer Hilary Bird

First published in 2012
by Ryland Peters & Small
20–21 Jockey's Fields
London WC1R 4BW
and
519 Broadway, 5th Floor
New York NY 10012

www.rylandpeters.com

Text © Ghillie Başan, Susannah Blake, Ross Dobson,
Tonia George, Brian Glover, Jennifer Joyce, Laura
Washburn and Ryland Peters & Small 2012

Design and photographs © Ryland Peters
& Small 2012

UK ISBN: 978-1-84975-254-1
10 9 8 7 6

US ISBN: 978-1-84975-283-1
10 9 8

A CIP record for this book is available from
the British Library.

US Library of Congress Cataloging-in-Publication
data has been applied for.

Printed and bound in China

Notes:
• All spoon measurements are level, unless
otherwise specified.
• Ovens should be preheated to the specified
temperature. Recipes in this book were tested
using a regular oven. If using a fan-assisted
oven, follow the manufacturer's instructions
for adjusting temperatures.
• All eggs are medium UK/large US, unless
otherwise specified. Recipes containing raw or
partially cooked egg should not be served to the
very young, very old, anyone with a compromised
immune system or pregnant women.

CONTENTS

THE SECRETS OF TAGINES

Colourful, decorative, scented and a feast for the senses – the food of Morocco reflects a fascinating mix of the cultures that have left their mark on the region: the indigenous Berbers with their tradition of tagine cooking and couscous; the nomadic Bedouins from the desert who brought dates, milk and grains; the Moors expelled from Spain who relied heavily on olives and olive oil and brought with them the Andalusian flavours of paprika and herbs; the Sephardic Jews with their preserving techniques employing salt; the Arabs who introduced the sophisticated cuisine from the Middle East; the Ottoman influence of kebabs/kabobs and pastry making; and finally, the finesse of the French.

The root of Moroccan cooking can be traced back to the indigenous Berber tribes. Steeped in tradition, the rural Berbers are proud of their ancestry. They have lived in North Africa, between Egypt and the western coast of Morocco, as far back as archaeological records go. Originally farmers, living alongside the nomadic Taureg and Bedouin tribes of the desert, the Berbers would have made an impact on the food of the region long before the invasion of the Arabs and, although they had to convert from Christianity to Islam and adopt new religious and culinary customs, they are keen to make the point that they are not of Arab descent. Many rural Berber communities speak their own languages and

It is Berbers we have to thank for tagines and couscous. A tagine is a glorified stew worthy of poetry – aromatic and syrupy, zesty and spicy, or sweet and fragrant are just some of the words that come to mind. It is a dish of tender meat, fish or succulent vegetables, simmered to perfection in buttery sauces with fruit, herbs, honey and chillies/chiles. An authentic tagine is in a class of its own and has become a fundamental feature of Moroccan cuisine.

The name 'tagine' (sometimes spelled 'tajine') is also given to the vessel in which the food is cooked: a shallow, round, earthenware pot with a unique conical lid designed to lock in moisture and flavours. In it, the food cooks gently in a small amount of liquid. The finished dish can either be served piping hot straight from its cooking vessel, or tipped into one of the decorative versions of the pot, glazed in beautiful shades of blue and green, to take to the table.

Although originally a Berber dish, the tagine has evolved with the history of the region as waves of Arab and Ottoman invaders, Moorish refugees from Andalusia and French colonialists have left their influences on the cuisine. Classic tagines include combinations of lamb with dried prunes or apricots; chicken with preserved lemon and green olives; duck with dates and honey; and fish cooked with tomatoes, lime and fresh coriander/cilantro. In the modern Maghreb, the Berbers are still renowned for their tasty, pungent tagines made with lots of onions and smen, a rancid clarified butter (see page 14) which is very much an acquired taste! The method employed in tagine cooking also varies from

dialects but those who are literate also speak Arabic and, in some areas, French. Berbers also fiercely uphold some of their own culinary customs, such as the festive pilgrimages, moussems, which are held in tented enclosures where traditional dishes, such as couscous, are cooked in vast quantities and shared. Another feature of Berber culinary life is the diffa, which is a festive banquet, varying in content in accordance with the wealth of the family, to mark special family occasions such as weddings, births and religious events.

the countryside to the cities. In the north, in cities like Tangier and Casablanca, where the Spanish and French influences are evident, the meat is often browned in butter or oil and the spices and onions are sautéed before adding the rest of the ingredients, whereas Fassi and Marrakchi tagines are often prepared by putting all the ingredients together in water and then adding extra butter or smen towards the end of the cooking time.

Traditionally, tagines are served as a course on their own, with freshly baked flat breads or crusty bread to mop up the delectable syrupy sauces, and are followed by a mound of couscous. The more modern way is to combine the courses and serve them with an accompanying salad or vegetable side dish. On festive occasions, the custom is to pile up a huge pyramid of couscous and hollow out the peak to form a well into which the tagine is spooned. However, most earthenware tagines are not big enough to cope with feasts, so large copper pots are often used instead.

The great secret of an authentic tagine is to simmer the ingredients over a low heat, so that everything remains deliciously moist and tender. Meat tagines may be cooked for several hours, the meat simmering gently in a seasoned, fragrant liquid until it is so tender it almost falls off the bone. Generally, dishes of vegetables, pulses or fish do not require long cooking times but still benefit from the tagine method in terms of enhanced taste and texture. Traditionally, tagines are cooked over a clay stove, or brazier, which is stoked with charcoal to maintain constant heat. Such stoves diffuse the heat around the base of the tagine, enabling the

liquid to reduce and thicken without drying out. Wood-burning ovens and open fires are used, too. However, wonderful tagines can also be produced using a modern stove or oven. Most authentic tagines have a little hole at the top of the conical lid to release some of the steam, so that it doesn't try to escape at the seam between the base and the lid. If there is no hole, you will probably need at intervals to tilt the lid at an angle to release the steam yourself. When cooking in an oven, it is generally only the base of the tagine that is used.

When it comes to buying a tagine, there are several different types and sizes, as some represent a Berber tribe, a particular village or a region of Morocco. There are a number of cooking tagines to choose from, but few of them come with a warning about their vulnerability over a conventional gas or electric stove. Most of the factory-made vessels, whether they are glazed or not, tend to form hairline cracks when they are placed over a gas flame and they cannot be used on an electric ring. For a glazed earthenware tagine, a heat diffuser is essential, otherwise it is worth splashing out on the durable cast-iron version with a glazed, earthenware lid produced by Le Creuset. Their version looks just like a beautifully authentic glazed tagine but the cast-iron base enables it to be used safely on gas or electric stoves. A solid, heavy-based casserole dish is a good substitute, as long as you keep the heat very low. But for a delicious meal, full of flavour and adventure, it is well worth attempting to cook with the genuine article.

10 unwaxed lemons, preferably the small, thin-skinned Meyer variety

10 tablespoons sea salt

freshly squeezed juice of 3–4 lemons

Makes 1 large jar

preserved lemons

Added to dishes as a refreshing, tangy ingredient or garnish, preserved lemons are essential to the cooking of tagines. You can buy jars of ready-preserved lemons in specialist shops and some supermarkets, but it is worth making your own.

Wash and dry the lemons and slice the ends off each one. Stand each lemon on one end and make two vertical cuts three-quarters of the way through them, as if cutting them into quarters but keeping the base intact. Stuff 1 tablespoon salt into each lemon and pack them into a large sterilized jar. Seal the jar and store the lemons in a cool place for 3–4 days to soften the skins.

Press the lemons down into the jar, so they are even more tightly packed. Pour the lemon juice over the salted lemons, until they are completely covered. Seal the jar again and store it in a cool place for at least 1 month. Rinse the salt off the preserved lemons before using.

smen (aged butter)

500 g/4 sticks plus 2 tablespoons unsalted butter, at room temperature

1 tablespoon sea salt

1 tablespoon dried oregano

Makes about 500 g/1 lb 2 oz.

This pungent butter, used as the primary cooking fat in some tagines, is left to mature in earthenware pots for months, sometimes years! You can substitute it with ghee (clarified butter).

Soften the butter in a bowl. Boil 150 ml/scant ⅔ cup water in a saucepan with the salt and oregano to reduce it a little, then strain it directly onto the butter. Stir the butter with a wooden spoon to make sure it is well blended, then let cool.

Knead the butter with your hands to bind it, squeezing out any excess water. Drain well and spoon the butter into a hot, sterilized jar. Seal the jar and store it in a cool, dry place for at least 6 weeks.

harissa paste

8 dried red chillies/chiles (Horn or New Mexico), deseeded

2–3 garlic cloves, finely chopped

½ teaspoon sea salt

1 teaspoon ground cumin

1 teaspoon ground coriander

4 tablespoons olive oil

Makes about 4 tablespoons

This fiery paste is popular throughout North Africa. It can be served as a condiment, or as a dip for warm crusty bread, and it can be stirred into tagines and couscous to impart its distinctive spicy taste. This recipe is for the basic paste, to which other ingredients such as fennel seeds, fresh coriander/cilantro and mint can be added. Jars of ready-prepared harissa are available in some supermarkets and at specialist deli counters but it's easy to make your own.

Put the chillies/chiles in a bowl and pour over enough warm water to cover them. Leave them to soak for 1 hour. Drain and squeeze out any excess water. Using a mortar and pestle, pound them to a paste with the garlic and salt (or whizz them in an electric mixer). Beat in the cumin and coriander and bind with the olive oil.

Store the harissa in a sealed jar in the refrigerator with a thin layer of olive oil poured on top. It will keep well for about 1 month.

ras-el-hanout

There is no one recipe for ras-el-hanout, a lovely pungent spice mix, packed with strong Indian aromas of cinnamon, cloves and ginger combined with local African roots and the delicate, perfumed notes of rosebuds. Every family has its own favourite blend. Some of the spices are available only in the Maghreb, so if your tagine recipe calls for this flavouring, your easiest solution is to select one of the ready-prepared spice mixes available in Middle Eastern and African stores. Alternatively, you could try this version.

1 teaspoon black peppercorns

1 teaspoon cloves

1 teaspoon aniseeds

1 teaspoon nigella seeds

1 teaspoon allspice berries

1 teaspoon cardamom seeds

2 teaspoons ground ginger

2 teaspoons ground turmeric

2 teaspoons coriander seeds

2 pieces mace

2 pieces cinnamon bark

2 teaspoons dried mint

1 dried red chilli/chile

1 teaspoon dried lavender

6 dried rosebuds, broken up

Makes about
4–5 tablespoons

Using a mortar and pestle, or an electric blender, grind together all the spices to form a coarse powder.

Stir in the lavender and rosebuds and tip the mixture into an airtight container.

You can store this spice mix for up to 6 months if you keep it in a cool cupboard and well away from direct sunlight.

TRADITIONAL
LAMB TAGINES

lamb tagine with prunes, apricots and honey

1–2 tablespoons ghee, or
1 tablespoon olive oil plus
1 tablespoon butter

2 tablespoons blanched almonds

2 red onions, finely chopped

2–3 garlic cloves, finely chopped

a thumb-sized piece of fresh
ginger, peeled and chopped

a pinch of saffron threads

2 cinnamon sticks

1–2 teaspoons coriander seeds,
crushed

500 g/1 lb. 2 oz. boned lamb,
from the shoulder, leg or shanks,
trimmed and cubed

12 dried, pitted prunes, soaked
for 1 hour and drained

6 dried, pitted apricots, soaked
for 1 hour and drained

3–4 strips orange zest

1–2 tablespoons dark, clear honey

leaves from a small bunch of
fresh coriander/cilantro leaves,
finely chopped

sea salt and freshly ground
black pepper

salad and crusty bread, to serve

Serves 4

A classic lamb tagine, sweetened with honey and fruit, is the perfect introduction to the tastes of Morocco. Traditionally, this aromatic dish is served with bread to soak up the syrupy sauce. To balance the sweetness, you could also serve a crunchy salad of finely shredded carrot, onions and cabbage or bell peppers.

Heat the ghee in a tagine or heavy-based casserole dish, stir in the almonds and cook until they turn golden. Add the onions and garlic and sauté until they begin to colour. Stir in the ginger, saffron, cinnamon sticks and coriander seeds. Toss in the lamb, making sure it is coated in the onion and spices, and sauté for 1–2 minutes.

Pour in enough water to just cover the meat and bring it to the boil. Reduce the heat, cover the tagine or casserole dish and simmer for about 1 hour, until the meat is tender. Add the prunes, apricots and orange zest, cover the tagine again, and simmer for a further 15–20 minutes. Stir in the honey, season with salt and pepper to taste, cover and simmer for a further 10 minutes. Make sure there is enough liquid in the pot, as you want the sauce to be syrupy and slightly caramelized, but not too dry – add a little more water if necessary.

Stir in some of the coriander/cilantro and reserve the rest to sprinkle over the top of the dish. Serve immediately with a salad and some crusty bread.

2–3 tablespoons ghee, or
1 tablespoon olive oil plus
1 tablespoon butter

2 onions, finely chopped

1–2 teaspoons ground turmeric

1 teaspoon ground ginger

2 teaspoons ground cinnamon

1 kg/2 lbs. 4 oz. lean, boned lamb,
from the shoulder, neck or leg,
trimmed and cubed

250 g/1¼ cups ready-to-eat
pitted dates

1 tablespoon dark, clear honey

1 tablespoon olive oil

1 tablespoon butter

2–3 tablespoons blanched
almonds

2 tablespoons shelled pistachios

leaves from a small bunch of
fresh flat leaf parsley, finely
chopped

sea salt and freshly ground
black pepper

Plain, Buttery Couscous
(see page 103), to serve

Serves 4

lamb tagine with dates, almonds and pistachios

In Arab culture, dates are an age-old source of nutrition and natural sugar; nomads could survive in the desert with dates alone for nourishment. As the fruit is regarded as special, it is often added to festive grain dishes and stews. This slightly sticky date and nut tagine is a favourite at weddings and other family feasts.

Heat the ghee in a tagine or heavy-based casserole dish. Stir in the onions and sauté until golden brown. Stir in the turmeric, ginger and cinnamon. Toss in the meat, making sure it is coated in the spice mixture. Pour in enough water to almost cover the meat and bring it to the boil. Reduce the heat, cover with a lid and simmer gently for roughly 1½ hours.

Add the dates and stir in the honey. Cover with a lid again and simmer for another 30 minutes. Season with salt and lots of black pepper.

Heat the olive oil with the butter in a small pan. Stir in the almonds and pistachios and cook until they begin to turn golden brown.

Scatter the toasted nuts over the lamb and dates and sprinkle with the flat leaf parsley. Serve with Plain, Buttery Couscous.

Commonly known as the 'bread of the desert', dates are treated as a sacred food source by the Arabs and the Berbers, as they and their ancestors have survived off them for generations, even when there has been little else to eat. Dates also symbolize hospitality and prosperity, so they are offered to guests and are used in numerous tagines and couscous dishes.

lamb tagine with shallots and dates

3 tablespoons ghee, or
2 tablespoons olive oil plus
1 tablespoon butter

700 g/1 lb. 9 oz. lean, boned lamb, from the shoulder or neck, trimmed and cubed

12 shallots, peeled and left whole

4–6 garlic cloves, peeled and left whole

2 teaspoons ground turmeric

2 cinnamon sticks

1–2 tablespoons dark, clear honey

225 g/1 cup ready-to-eat pitted dates

1–2 tablespoons sesame seeds, toasted

sea salt and freshly ground black pepper

crusty bread or Plain, Buttery Couscous (see page 103), to serve

Serves 4

Heat the ghee in a tagine or heavy-based casserole dish. Toss in the lamb and brown it all over. Using a slotted spoon, remove the meat from the tagine and set aside. Add the shallots and garlic and sauté, stirring occasionally, until they begin to colour.

Add the turmeric and cinnamon sticks and return the meat to the tagine. Pour in just enough water to cover the meat then bring it to the boil. Reduce the heat, cover with the lid and simmer for about 1 hour, stirring occasionally.

Stir in the honey and season with salt and plenty of black pepper. Add the dates, replace the lid, and cook for 25–30 minutes.

Sprinkle with the toasted sesame seeds and serve with crusty bread or Plain, Buttery Couscous.

baked lamb tagine with quinces, figs and honey

1.5 kg/3 lbs. 5 oz. shoulder of lamb on the bone

2 tablespoons ghee, or 1 tablespoon olive oil plus 1 tablespooon butter

2 red onions, cut into wedges

225 g/1 cup ready-to-eat pitted prunes

225 g/1½ cups ready-to-eat dried figs, or fresh figs, halved

40 g/3 tablespoons butter

2 fresh quinces, quartered

2–3 tablespoons orange flower water

2 tablespoons dark, clear honey

leaves from a small bunch of fresh flat leaf parsley, chopped

leaves from a small bunch of fresh coriander/cilantro, chopped

Plain, Buttery Couscous (see page 103) or roasted potatoes, to serve

FOR THE CHERMOULA:

2–3 garlic cloves, chopped

1 fresh red chilli/chile, chopped

1 teaspoon sea salt

a small bunch of fresh coriander/cilantro

a pinch of saffron threads

1–2 teaspoons ground cumin

3–4 tablespoons olive oil

freshly squeezed juice of 1 lemon

Serves 4–6

In this festive dish, a shoulder of lamb is marinated in chermoula – a delicious Moroccan herb and spice mix – and baked slowly. If you have difficulty sourcing quinces, you can use sharp green apples or pears instead.

To make the chermoula, use a mortar and pestle to pound the garlic and chilli/chile with the salt to form a paste. Add the coriander/cilantro leaves and pound to a coarse paste. Beat in the saffron and cumin and bind with the oil and lemon juice.

Cut small incisions in the shoulder of lamb with a sharp knife and rub the chermoula well into the meat. Cover and leave in the refrigerator for at least 6 hours, or overnight.

Preheat the oven to 180°C (350°F) Gas 4.

Heat the ghee in a tagine or heavy-based casserole dish, add the lamb and brown it all over. Transfer the meat to a plate. Stir the onions and any leftover chermoula into the ghee. Add the prunes and if using dried figs, add them at this stage. Pour in 300 ml/1⅓ cups water and put the lamb back into the tagine. Cover and bake in the oven for 2 hours.

Towards the end of the cooking time, melt the butter in a heavy-based pan, toss in the quinces and sauté until golden brown. Remove the tagine from the oven and place the golden quinces around the meat (if using fresh figs, add them at this stage). Add the orange flower water and honey. Return the tagine to the oven for a further 25–30 minutes, until the lamb is so tender it almost falls off the bone. Sprinkle the chopped parsley and coriander/cilantro over the top and serve immediately with Plain, Buttery Couscous or roasted potatoes.

lamb tagine with chestnuts, saffron and pomegranate seeds

2 tablespoons ghee, or
1 tablespoon olive oil plus
1 tablespoon butter

2 onions, finely chopped

4 garlic cloves, finely chopped

thumb-sized piece of fresh ginger, peeled and finely chopped or shredded

a pinch of saffron threads

1–2 cinnamon sticks

1 kg/2 lbs. 4 oz. lean, boned lamb, from the shoulder or leg, trimmed and cubed

250 g/2 cups peeled chestnuts

1–2 tablespoons dark, clear honey

seeds of 1 pomegranate, pith removed

leaves from a small bunch of fresh mint, chopped

leaves from a small bunch of fresh coriander/cilantro, chopped

sea salt and freshly ground black pepper

crusty bread or Plain, Buttery Couscous (see page 103), to serve

Serves 4–6

This is a lovely winter dish, decorated with jewel-like ruby-red pomegranate seeds. Whole, meaty chestnuts are often used in Arab-influenced culinary cultures as a substitute for potatoes. You can use freshly roasted nuts or ready-peeled, vacuum-packed or frozen chestnuts.

Heat the ghee in a tagine or heavy-based casserole dish. Stir in the onions, garlic and ginger and sauté until they begin to colour. Add the saffron and cinnamon sticks, and toss in the lamb. Pour in enough water to almost cover the meat and bring it to the boil. Reduce the heat, cover with a lid and simmer gently for about 1 hour.

Add the chestnuts and stir in the honey. Cover with the lid again and cook gently for a further 30 minutes, until the meat is very tender.

Season to taste with salt and plenty of black pepper and then toss in some of the pomegranate seeds, mint and coriander/cilantro. Sprinkle the remaining pomegranate seeds and herbs over the lamb, and serve with Plain, Buttery Couscous.

tfaia tagine with onions, browned almonds and eggs

1–2 tablespoons ghee or smen (see page 14) or 1 tablespoon olive oil plus 1 tablespoon butter

2 garlic cloves, crushed

1 teaspoon ground ginger

1 teaspoon ground coriander

1 teaspoon saffron threads, ground with a pinch of salt

1 kg/2 lbs. 4 oz. lamb cutlets

2 onions, finely chopped

175 g/1¼ cups black Kalamata olives, pitted

2 preserved lemons (see page 13), cut into quarters

leaves from a small bunch of fresh coriander/cilantro, chopped

sea salt and freshly ground black pepper

TO SERVE:

4 eggs

½ teaspoon ground saffron, or a pinch of saffron threads

½ tablespoon ghee or butter

2 tablespoons blanched almonds

crusty bread

Serves 4

Originally from Andalusia, tfaia tagines are popular in northern Morocco, particularly in Tangier. Their trademark is a pungent, nutty flavour that emanates from matured, clarified butter called smen, which is an acquired taste for some people. The recipe works just as well with ghee, which is ordinary clarified butter.

Melt the ghee in a tagine or heavy-based casserole dish. Stir in the garlic, ginger, ground coriander and saffron, and roll the lamb cutlets in the mixture. Sprinkle the onions over the cutlets and pour in just enough water to cover the meat. Bring the water to the boil, reduce the heat, cover with a lid and cook gently for about 1½ hours.

Add the olives and lemons and cook, uncovered, for about another 20 minutes to reduce the sauce. Season well with plenty of salt and black pepper and toss in the chopped coriander/cilantro.

Meanwhile, boil the eggs in their shells for about 4 minutes, so that the yolk is just firm, and shell them. Dissolve the saffron in 2 tablespoons warm water and roll the eggs in the yellow liquid to colour them. Cut the eggs in half lengthways.

In a frying pan, melt the ghee and stir in the almonds until golden brown. Sprinkle the toasted almonds over the tagine and arrange the eggs around the edge. Serve immediately with crusty bread.

tagine of lamb and vegetables with mint

3–4 tablespoons olive oil

1 onion, roughly chopped

4 garlic cloves, roughly chopped

1 teaspoon cumin seeds

1 teaspoon coriander seeds

1 teaspoon dried mint

thumb-sized piece of fresh ginger, peeled and finely chopped or grated

750 g/1 lb. 10 oz. lean, boned lamb, from the shoulder or leg, trimmed and cubed

2 small courgettes/zucchini, sliced thickly on the diagonal

1 red or yellow bell pepper, deseeded and cut into thick strips

4 tomatoes, skinned, deseeded and cut into chunks

leaves from a small bunch of fresh flat leaf parsley, roughly chopped

leaves from a small bunch of fresh mint, roughly chopped

sea salt and freshly ground black pepper

1 lemon, cut into quarters, to serve

Serves 4

Summer tagines using seasonal vegetables are often quite light and colourful. Other vegetables that might be added to this tagine include tomatoes, aubergines/eggplant and peas. This dish is particularly good served with wedges of lemon to squeeze over it, or topped with finely shredded preserved lemon.

Heat the olive oil in a tagine or heavy-based casserole dish. Stir in the onion, garlic, cumin and coriander seeds, dried mint and ginger. Once the onions begin to soften, toss in the meat and pour in enough water to just cover it. Bring the water to the boil, reduce the heat, cover with a lid and cook gently for about 1½ hours.

Season the cooking juices with salt and pepper. Add the courgettes/zucchini, pepper and tomatoes, tucking them around the meat (add a little more water if necessary). Cover with a lid again and cook for about 15 minutes, until the courgettes/zucchini and pepper are cooked but retain a bite.

Toss in some of the chopped parsley and mint, sprinkle the rest over the top and serve immediately with lemon wedges on the side to squeeze over the dish.

lamb k'dra with sweet potatoes and okra

6–8 lamb shanks, boned, trimmed and cut into bite-sized pieces

6 onions, halved lengthways and sliced crossways

a pinch of saffron threads

2 cinnamon sticks

1 teaspoon ground black pepper

2 sweet potatoes, peeled, halved lengthways and thickly sliced

2 tablespoons ghee, smen (see page 14) or butter

250 g/2½ cups fresh okra

freshly squeezed juice of 1 lemon

sea salt

crusty bread or Plain, Buttery Couscous (see page 103), to serve

Serves 6–8

This is a Berber dish that is often prepared with large cuts of meat, such as shanks, knuckle or sheeps' heads, which are removed at the end of the cooking and arranged around a mound of couscous. The vegetables are served on top and the cooking broth is served separately to spoon over the dish.

Put the lamb in a tagine or large heavy-based casserole dish with half the onions and all the saffron, cinnamon sticks and black pepper. Pour in enough water to cover the meat and bring to the boil. Reduce the heat, cover with a lid and simmer gently for 1½ hours (top up with water if needed).

Add the sweet potatoes, the ghee and the rest of the onions. Simmer for a further 20–25 minutes, until the potatoes are tender. Meanwhile, toss the okra in the lemon juice, leave for 10 minutes, then drain. Add the okra to the casserole dish and simmer for a further 5–10 minutes, until the okra is cooked through but still retains a crunch.

Season to taste with salt and serve with crusty bread or Plain, Buttery Couscous.

BEEF, KEFTA AND SAUSAGE TAGINES

beef tagine with oranges

1–2 tablespoons ghee, or
1 tablespoon olive oil plus
1 tablespoon butter

3–4 garlic cloves, crushed

1 red onion, halved and sliced

5 cm/2 inches fresh ginger, peeled
and finely chopped or grated

1 fresh red chilli/chile, deseeded
and sliced

2 teaspoons coriander seeds,
crushed

2 cinnamon sticks

3–4 beetroot/beets, peeled and
quartered

500 g/1 lb. 2 oz. lean beef, cubed
or cut into strips

2 thin-skinned oranges, cut into
segments

1 tablespoon dark, clear honey

1–2 tablespoons orange
flower water

1 tablespoon butter

2–3 tablespoons shelled pistachios

leaves from a small bunch of fresh
flat leaf parsley, roughly chopped

sea salt and freshly ground
black pepper

Plain, Buttery Couscous
(see page 103), to serve

Serves 4

Earthy and fruity with a hint of ginger, this tagine is a good winter warmer. It can be made with either fresh or pre-cooked beetroot/beets. You could serve it with roasted butternut squash and a mound of Plain, Buttery Couscous tossed with pistachios.

Melt the ghee in a tagine or heavy-based casserole dish, add the garlic, onion and ginger and stir until they begin to colour. Add the chilli/chile, coriander seeds and cinnamon sticks. Add the beetroot/beets and sauté for 2–3 minutes. Toss in the beef and sauté for 1 minute. Pour in enough water to almost cover the beef and beetroot/beets and bring to the boil. Reduce the heat, cover with a lid and simmer for 1 hour, until the meat is very tender.

Add the orange segments, honey and orange flower water to the tagine and season to taste with salt and pepper. Cover with the lid and cook for a further 10–15 minutes.

Melt the butter in a small saucepan and toss in the pistachios, stirring them over medium heat until they turn golden brown. Sprinkle them over the tagine along with the flat leaf parsley and serve immediately with Plain, Buttery Couscous.

beef tagine with sweet potatoes, peas, ginger and ras-el-hanout

2 tablespoons ghee or smen (see page 14), or 1 tablespoon olive oil plus 1 tablespoon butter

5 cm/2 inches fresh ginger, peeled and finely shredded

1 onion, finely chopped

1 kg/2 lbs. 4 oz. lean beef, cut into bite-sized pieces

1–2 teaspoons ras-el-hanout (see page 18)

2 sweet potatoes, peeled and cubed

500 g/3½ cups fresh or frozen peas

2–3 tomatoes, skinned, deseeded and chopped

1 preserved lemon (see page 13), finely shredded or chopped

leaves from a small bunch of fresh coriander/cilantro, finely chopped

sea salt and freshly ground black pepper

crusty bread and plain yogurt, to serve

Serves 4

This fairly fiery dish is laced with the powerful flavours and aromas of ras-el-hanout, a traditional spice mix. Regional variations use turnip, yam, pumpkin or butternut squash instead of sweet potatoes. It is best served with chunks of crusty bread and cooling yogurt or a glass of mint tea.

Heat the ghee in a tagine or heavy-based casserole dish. Add in the ginger and onion and sauté until soft. Toss in the beef and sear it on all sides, then stir in the ras-el-hanout. Pour in enough water to just cover the meat and bring it to the boil. Reduce the heat, cover with the lid and cook gently for about 40 minutes.

Add the sweet potato to the tagine, season to taste with salt and pepper, cover and cook gently for a further 20 minutes, until the meat is tender. Toss in the peas and tomatoes, cover and cook for a further 5–10 minutes.

Sprinkle the preserved lemon and chopped coriander/cilantro over the top and serve immediately with crusty bread and plain yogurt.

kefta tagine with eggs and roasted cumin

225 g/8 oz. finely minced/ground lamb

1 onion, finely chopped

1 teaspoon dried mint

1–2 teaspoons ras-el-hanout (see page 18)

½ teaspoon cayenne pepper

leaves from a small bunch of fresh flat leaf parsley, finely chopped

1 tablespoon butter

¼–½ teaspoon salt

1 teaspoon cayenne pepper or ½ teaspoon dried chilli/hot pepper flakes

4 eggs

1–2 teaspoons cumin seeds, dry-roasted and ground

leaves from a small bunch of fresh flat leaf parsley, roughly chopped

sea salt and freshly ground black pepper

crusty bread and plain yogurt, to serve

Serves 4

Variations of this great street dish can be found throughout the Maghreb. It is also often prepared as a snack in the home. In many households, kefta (poached meatballs) are prepared in batches and stored in the refrigerator. Kefta are usually quite fiery, so serve them with plenty of good bread and plain yogurt to temper their hotness.

To make the kefta, put the lamb, onion, mint, ras-el-hanout, cayenne pepper and parsley in a bowl. Season to taste with salt and pepper and mix well together. Using your hands, knead the mixture and mould it into small walnut-sized balls, so that you end up with about 12 balls.

Fill a tagine or heavy-based casserole dish with water and bring it to the boil. Carefully drop in the kefta, a few at a time, and poach them for about 10 minutes, turning them so that they are cooked on all sides. Remove them with a slotted spoon and drain on kitchen paper. Reserve roughly 300 ml/1¼ cups of the cooking liquid. (If not using the kefta immediately, transfer them to a plate to cool and store, covered, in the refrigerator for 2–3 days.)

Add the butter to the reserved cooking liquid in the tagine and bring the mixture to the boil. Stir in the salt and cayenne pepper and drop in the poached kefta. Cook over high heat until almost all the liquid has evaporated. Carefully crack the eggs around the kefta, cover with a lid and leave the eggs to cook in the sauce and steam until they are just set.

Sprinkle the roasted cumin and chopped parsley over the top of the dish and serve immediately with crusty bread and plain yogurt.

450 g/1 lb. finely minced/ground lamb

1 onion, finely chopped or grated

leaves from a small bunch of fresh flat leaf parsley, finely chopped

1–2 teaspoons ground cinnamon

1 teaspoon ground cumin

1 teaspoon ground coriander

½ teaspoon cayenne pepper

sea salt and freshly ground black pepper

1 tablespoon each olive oil and butter

1 onion, roughly chopped

2–3 garlic cloves, halved and crushed

5 cm/2 inches fresh ginger, peeled and finely chopped

1 red chilli/chile, thinly sliced

2 teaspoons ground turmeric

leaves from a small bunch of fresh coriander/cilantro, chopped

leaves from a small bunch of fresh mint, chopped

freshly squeezed juice of 1 lemon

1 lemon, cut into wedges

Plain, Buttery Couscous (see page 103), tossed with chopped red chilli/chile and fresh herbs, to serve

Serves 4

spicy kefta tagine with lemon

Kefta tagines don't require long cooking times, as generally the sauce is made first and the meatballs are poached in it. This popular recipe is light and lemony and delicious served with Plain, Buttery Couscous tossed with chilli/chile and herbs and a leafy green salad.

To make the kefta, put the lamb in a bowl with the onion, parsley, cinnamon, cumin, coriander and cayenne, and season to taste with salt and black pepper. Using your hands, knead the mixture and mould it into small walnut-sized balls, so that you end up with about 16 balls. (These can be made ahead of time and kept in the refrigerator for 2–3 days.)

Heat the oil and butter in a tagine or heavy-based casserole dish. Stir in the onion, garlic, ginger and chilli/chile and sauté until they begin to brown. Add the turmeric and half the coriander/cilantro and mint, and pour in 300 ml/1¼ cups water. Bring to the boil, reduce the heat and simmer, covered, for 10 minutes. Carefully place the kefta in the liquid, cover and poach for about 15 minutes, rolling them in the liquid from time to time so they are cooked well on all sides. Pour over the lemon juice, season the liquid with salt and tuck the lemon wedges around the kefta. Poach for a further 10 minutes.

Sprinkle with the remaining coriander/cilantro and mint and serve with Plain, Buttery Couscous tossed with chilli/chile and herbs.

chickpea and chorizo tagine with bay leaves, paprika and sage

175 g/scant 1 cup dried
chickpeas, soaked overnight
in plenty of water

2–3 tablespoons olive oil

2 red onions, halved and sliced

2 garlic cloves, chopped

1 thin chorizo, roughly 15 cm/
6 inches long, sliced on the
diagonal, or 450 g/1 lb. merguez
sausages

2–3 fresh bay leaves

several sprigs of fresh thyme

1–2 teaspoons Spanish smoked
paprika (pimentòn)

leaves from a small bunch of
fresh sage, shredded

freshly squeezed juice of 1 lemon

sea salt and freshly ground
black pepper

warmed flat breads and plain
yogurt, to serve

Serves 4

This is a classic, Spanish-influenced peasant dish, which is often eaten on its own with plain yogurt and bread, but is also served with grilled or roasted meats, such as lamb chops. Either chorizo or Moroccan merguez sausages can be used, as both impart their spicy flavours to the dish. For a meatless version, just omit the sausage, as the chickpeas are extremely tasty on their own.

Drain the chickpeas, put them in a large saucepan and cover with plenty of water. Bring the water to the boil, reduce the heat and simmer for 45 minutes or until the chickpeas are soft but still have a bite to them. Drain well and refresh under cold running water. Remove any loose skins and discard them.

Heat the olive oil in a tagine or heavy-based casserole dish. Stir in the onions and garlic and sauté until they begin to colour. Add the chorizo, bay leaves and thyme and sauté until lightly browned. Toss in the chickpeas, add the paprika and cover with a lid. Cook gently for 10–15 minutes, to allow the flavours to mingle.

Add in the sage leaves and lemon juice and gently toss. Season to taste with salt and pepper and serve hot with warmed flat breads and plain yogurt.

chorizo tagine with lentils and fenugreek

This is very simple yet delicious peasant food. Prepared with locally cured, spicy Moroccan merguez sausages or chorizo and lentils or beans, it is a satisfying dish, best served with flat breads and a generous dollop of creamy yogurt.

2 tablespoons olive oil

2 onions, chopped

2 garlic cloves, chopped

450 g/1 lb. chorizo or merguez sausages, thickly sliced

2 teaspoons ground turmeric

2 teaspoons ground fenugreek

225 g/1 cup brown lentils

1 x 400-g/14-oz. can chopped tomatoes

2 teaspoons sugar

leaves from a bunch of fresh coriander/cilantro, roughly chopped (reserve some to garnish)

sea salt and freshly ground black pepper

warmed flat breads and plain yogurt, to serve

Serves 4–6

Heat the oil in a tagine or heavy-based casserole dish. Add the onions and garlic and sauté until they begin to colour. Toss in the chorizo or merguez slices and sauté for 1–2 minutes just to flavour the oil. Stir in the turmeric and fenugreek and add the lentils, making sure they are well coated with the spices.

Add the tomatoes with the sugar and pour in enough water to cover the lentils by 2.5 cm/1 inch. Bring the liquid to the boil, reduce the heat, put on the lid and cook gently for about 25 minutes, adding more water if necessary, until the lentils are tender but not mushy.

Toss in the coriander/cilantro and season to taste with salt and pepper. Scatter the rest of the coriander/cilantro over the top and serve with warmed flat breads and plain yogurt.

CHICKEN AND
DUCK TAGINES

chicken tagine with preserved lemons, green olives and thyme

8–10 chicken thighs or
4 whole legs

2 tablespoons ghee or 1
tablespoon olive oil plus 1
tablespoon butter

2 preserved lemons (see page 13),
cut into strips

175 g/1 cup pitted green olives

1–2 teaspoons dried thyme or
oregano

steamed carrots tossed with
fresh mint, to serve (optional)

FOR THE MARINADE:

1 onion, grated

3 garlic cloves, crushed

5 cm/2 inches fresh ginger, peeled
and grated

leaves from a small bunch of
fresh coriander/cilantro, finely
chopped

a pinch of saffron threads

freshly squeezed juice of 1 lemon

1 teaspoon coarse sea salt

3–4 tablespoons olive oil

sea salt and freshly ground
black pepper

Serves 4

Preserved lemon and green olives are two of the principal ingredients of traditional Moroccan cooking. You can buy the olives at Middle Eastern and North African stores and some deli counters. The tagine can be made with chicken joints or a whole chicken. Serve with steamed carrots tossed with fresh mint.

First make the marinade. Mix all the ingredients for the marinade together in a small bowl. Put the chicken pieces in a shallow dish and coat them in the marinade, rubbing it into the skin. Cover and chill in the refrigerator for 1–2 hours.

Heat the olive oil with the butter in a tagine or heavy-based casserole dish. Remove the chicken pieces from the marinade and brown them in the oil. Pour over the marinade that is left in the dish and add enough water to come halfway up the sides of the chicken. Bring the water to the boil, reduce the heat, cover and simmer for about 45 minutes, turning the chicken from time to time.

Add the preserved lemons, olives and half the thyme to the tagine. Cover and simmer for a further 15–20 minutes. Season to taste with salt and pepper and sprinkle the remaining thyme over the top. Serve with steamed carrots tossed with fresh mint, if liked.

4 chicken breasts, cut into thick strips or chunks

2 tablespoons olive oil

2 onions, halved and sliced

½ preserved lemon (see page 13), thinly sliced

1–2 teaspoons sugar

1–2 teaspoons harissa paste (see page 17)

2 teaspoons tomato purée/paste

300 ml/1¼ cups chicken stock or water

1 x 400-g/14-oz. can artichoke hearts, drained, rinsed and halved

16 green grapes, halved lengthways

leaves from a bunch of fresh coriander/cilantro, coarsely chopped

sea salt and freshly ground black pepper

warmed flat breads, to serve

FOR THE MARINADE:

2 garlic cloves, crushed

1 teaspoon ground turmeric

freshly squeezed juice of 1 lemon

1 tablespoon olive oil

Serves 4

chicken tagine with harissa, artichokes and green grapes

With the tangy notes of preserved lemon combined with the sweet grapes, this tagine is deliciously refreshing and is best accompanied by warmed flat breads. This recipe uses ready-prepared canned artichoke hearts.

First, make the marinade. Mix all the ingredients together in a large bowl. Add the chicken breasts to the bowl and toss them in the mixture, then cover and leave in the refrigerator to marinate for 1–2 hours.

Heat the oil in a tagine or heavy-based casserole dish. Add the onions, preserved lemon and sugar and sauté for 2–3 minutes, until slightly caramelized. Toss in the marinated chicken, then add the harissa and tomato purée/paste. Pour in the stock and bring it to the boil. Reduce the heat, cover and simmer gently for 15 minutes.

Add the artichoke hearts, cover and cook for a further 5 minutes. Add the grapes with some of the coriander/cilantro and season to taste with salt and pepper. Sprinkle with the remaining coriander/cilantro and serve with warmed flat breads.

spicy chicken tagine with apricots, rosemary and ginger

2 tablespoons olive oil plus 1 tablespoon butter

1 onion, finely chopped

3 fresh rosemary sprigs, 1 finely chopped, the other 2 cut in half

7.5 cm/3 inches fresh ginger, peeled and finely chopped

2 fresh red chillies/chiles, deseeded and finely chopped

1–2 cinnamon sticks

8 chicken thighs

175 g/1 cup ready-to-eat dried apricots

2 tablespoons dark, clear honey

1 x 400-g/14-oz. can plum tomatoes with juice

leaves from a small bunch of fresh green or purple basil

sea salt and freshly ground black pepper

Plain, Buttery Couscous (see page 103), to serve

Serves 4

This tagine is both fruity and spicy, and the rosemary and ginger give it a delightful aroma. It can also be made with chicken joints or pigeon breasts, pheasant or duck, and needs only Plain, Buttery Couscous to accompany it.

Heat the oil and butter in a tagine or heavy-based casserole dish. Add the onion, chopped rosemary, ginger and chillies/chiles and sauté until the onion begins to soften.

Stir in the halved rosemary sprigs and the cinnamon sticks. Add the chicken thighs and brown them on both sides. Toss in the apricots with the honey, then stir in the plum tomatoes with their juice. (Add a little water if necessary, to ensure there is enough liquid to cover the base of the tagine and submerge the apricots.) Bring the liquid to the boil, then reduce the heat. Cover and simmer gently for 35–40 minutes, until the chicken is cooked through.

Season to taste with salt and pepper. Shred the larger basil leaves and leave the small ones intact. Sprinkle them over the chicken and serve with Plain, Buttery Couscous.

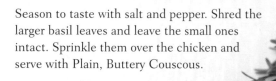

chicken k'dra with chickpeas, raisins and red peppers

A Moroccan k'dra is a stew cooked in the traditional fermented butter, smen (which gives it its distinctive taste), in a large copper pot (a k'dra). The other feature of a k'dra is the large quantity of onions used in the dish. A k'dra is best served on its own, perhaps with a little bread, and wedges of lemon to squeeze over it, or with a mound of Plain, Buttery Couscous.

1 chicken, about 1.5 kg/3 lbs. 5 oz., jointed into 6 pieces

175 g/scant 1 cup chickpeas, soaked in cold water for at least 6 hours and drained

6 onions, finely chopped

1–2 cinnamon sticks

2 pinches of saffron threads

1 teaspoon sea salt

1 teaspoon freshly ground black pepper

2 red bell peppers, left whole

3–4 tablespoons olive oil

3–4 tablespoons golden raisins or sultanas

2 tablespoons smen, ghee or butter (see page 14)

a bunch of fresh flat leaf parsley, finely chopped

1 lemon, cut into wedges, to serve

crusty bread or Plain, Buttery Couscous (see page 103), to serve

Serves 4–6

Put the chicken in a tagine or heavy-based casserole dish. Add the chickpeas, 2 tablespoons of the chopped onion, the cinnamon sticks and saffron strands and season with the salt and pepper. Pour in enough water to cover the chicken and chickpeas by 2.5 cm/1 inch and bring it to the boil. Cover the casserole dish , reduce the heat and cook gently for about 1 hour, checking the water level from time to time.

Meanwhile, preheat the oven to 180°C (350°F) Gas 4. Put the peppers in a baking dish and pour over the oil. Bake them in the preheated oven for about 30 minutes, until they are tender and the skin has buckled slightly. Remove them from the oven and leave them until they are cool enough to handle. Peel off the skin, cut the peppers in half lengthways, remove the stalk and seeds and cut the flesh into long strips. Set aside.

Check the chicken and chickpeas, both of which should be tender, and add the rest of the onions with the raisins, butter and half the parsley. Put the lid back on and cook gently for about 40 minutes, until the onions have almost formed a purée and there is very little liquid left.

Arrange the chicken joints on a serving dish and spoon the chickpeas, raisins and onions around them. Scatter the strips of pepper over the top and serve with lemon wedges to squeeze over and crusty bread or Plain, Buttery Couscous.

chicken k'dra with turnips and chickpeas

Traditionally cooked in a large copper pot, k'dra dishes are often packed with plenty of vegetables to create a hearty, filling dish for a big family or a large gathering of people.

1 kg/2 lb. 4 oz. chicken thighs

1–2 tablespoons ground turmeric

2–3 tablespoons olive oil plus 1 tablespoon butter

2 onions, coarsely chopped

4 garlic cloves, chopped

2–3 teaspoons coriander seeds

225 g/1¼ cups dried chickpeas, soaked for at least 6 hours in cold water and drained

450 g/1 lb. turnip flesh, cut into bite-sized pieces, or 8 baby turnips, halved

1 tablespoon smen, ghee or butter, melted (optional)

leaves from a bunch of fresh flat leaf parsley, coarsely chopped

sea salt and freshly ground black pepper

crusty bread, to serve

Serves 4–6

Trim the chicken thighs and rub them with the ground turmeric. Set aside.

Heat the oil and butter in a tagine or heavy-based casserole dish. Add the onions, garlic and coriander seeds and stir until they begin to colour.

Add the chicken thighs and brown lightly, then toss in the chickpeas and cover with 850 ml/scant 3½ cups water. Bring to the boil, reduce the heat, cover and simmer for about 45 minutes, until the chicken and chickpeas are tender.

Add the turnip and a little extra water if necessary and cook for a further 10–15 minutes, depending on the type of turnip, until cooked but still firm. Season to taste with salt and pepper, pour over the melted ghee, if using, and garnish with the chopped parsley. Serve with crusty bread.

tagine of duck breasts with dates, honey and orange flower water

5 cm/2 inches fresh ginger, peeled and chopped

2–3 garlic cloves, chopped

2–3 tablespoons olive oil plus 1 tablespoon butter

2 cinnamon sticks

4 duck breasts, on the bone

2–3 tablespoons dark, clear honey

225 g/1 cup ready-to-eat pitted dates

1–2 tablespoons orange flower water

1 tablespoon butter

2–3 tablespoons blanched almonds

sea salt and freshly ground black pepper

Plain, Buttery Couscous (see page 103) tossed with finely chopped preserved lemon (see page 13) and fresh green herbs, to serve

Serves 4

This traditional Moorish dish appears in various guises throughout the Arab-influenced world. Poultry cooked with dates and honey is probably one of the most ancient culinary combinations and the finished dish is deliciously succulent. You can substitute the duck with chicken, pigeon or poussins, if you prefer.

Using a mortar and pestle, pound the ginger and garlic to a paste. Heat the olive oil and butter in a tagine or heavy-based casserole dish, then stir in the ginger-garlic paste and the cinnamon sticks. Once the mixture begins to colour, add the duck breasts and brown the skin.

Stir in the honey and tuck the dates around the duck. Add enough water (the amount will vary according to the size of your tagine) to cover the base of the tagine and to come about one-third of the way up the duck breasts. Bring to the boil, reduce the heat and cover. Cook gently for about 25 minutes.

Add the orange flower water and season to taste with salt and pepper. Cover and cook for a further 5 minutes, or until the duck is tender.

In a frying pan, melt the butter and stir in the almonds. Sauté until golden brown and then scatter them over the duck. Serve immediately with Plain, Buttery Couscous flavoured with preserved lemon and herbs.

duck tagine with pears and cinnamon

2 tablespoons olive oil plus
1 tablespoon butter

2 onions, finely chopped

5 cm/2 inches fresh ginger,
peeled and finely chopped

2 cinnamon sticks

a pinch of saffron threads

1 kg/2 lb. 4 oz. boned duck meat,
from the thigh, breast or leg, cut
into bite-sized pieces

2 tablespoons butter

3–4 tablespoons dark, clear honey

3 pears, peeled, quartered
and cored

2–3 tablespoons orange
flower water

1–2 tablespoons toasted
sesame seeds

a few lemon balm leaves, to
garnish (optional)

sea salt and freshly ground
black pepper

crusty bread or Plain, Buttery
Couscous (see page 103),
to serve

Serves 4–6

*This traditional tagine can be prepared with duck, chicken,
poussin or quails. Variations of the recipe can include quince,
plums, apples, cherries and apricots. Serve the tagine with bread
to mop up the syrupy juices or with Plain, Buttery Couscous.*

Heat the oil and butter in a tagine or heavy-based saucepan. Add the
onions and ginger and sauté until they begin to colour, then add the
cinnamon sticks and saffron. Toss in the duck meat, making sure it is
well coated in the ginger and onions. Pour in roughly 600 ml/2½ cups
water and bring it to the boil. Reduce the heat, cover and simmer gently
for about 40 minutes, until the duck is tender.

Meanwhile, melt the butter in a heavy-based saucepan and stir in the
honey. Toss in the pears and cook gently until they begin to caramelize.
Add the pears to the duck with the orange flower water and cook the
tagine for a further 10 minutes.

Season to taste with salt and pepper and
scatter the roasted sesame seeds over
the top. Garnish with the lemon
balm leaves, if using, and serve
with crusty bread or Plain,
Buttery Couscous.

FISH AND
SEAFOOD TAGINES

1 quantity Chermoula
(see page 28)

900 g/2 lbs. fresh fish fillets,
such as cod or haddock, cut into
large chunks

2–3 tablespoons olive oil

1 red onion, finely chopped

2 carrots, finely chopped

2 celery stalks, finely chopped

1 preserved lemon (see page 13),
finely chopped

1 x 400-g/14-oz. can plum
tomatoes with their juice

150 ml/⅔ cup fish stock or water

150 ml/⅔ cup white wine or
fino sherry

sea salt and freshly ground
black pepper

leaves from a bunch of fresh
mint, finely shredded

Serves 4–6

fish tagine with preserved lemon and mint

The fish tagines of coastal Morocco are often made with whole fish, or with large chunks of fleshy fish such as sea bass, monkfish and cod. The fish is first marinated in a chermoula-style flavouring, and the dish is given an additional depth of flavour with a little white wine or sherry.

First, make the chermoula. Reserve 2 teaspoons of the mixture for cooking. Toss the fish chunks in the remaining chermoula, cover and leave to marinate in the refrigerator for 1–2 hours.

Heat the oil in a tagine or heavy-based casserole dish. Stir in the onion, carrots and celery and sauté until softened. Add the preserved lemon (reserving a little for sprinkling) with the reserved 2 teaspoons of chermoula and the tomatoes and stir in well. Cook gently for about 10 minutes to reduce the liquid, then add the stock and the wine or sherry. Bring the liquid to the boil, cover the tagine, reduce the heat and simmer for 10–15 minutes.

Toss the fish in the tagine, cover and cook gently for 6–8 minutes, until the fish is cooked through. Season to taste with salt and pepper, sprinkle with the reserved preserved lemon and the shredded mint leaves and serve immediately.

tagine of monkfish, potatoes, cherry tomatoes and black olives

1 quantity Chermoula
(see page 28)

900 g/2 lbs. monkfish tail,
cut into chunks

12 small new potatoes

3 tablespoons olive oil plus
1 tablespoon butter

3–4 garlic cloves, thinly sliced

12–16 cherry tomatoes

2 green peppers, grilled until
black, skinned and cut into strips

12 black olives

1 lemon, cut into wedges, to serve

sea salt and freshly ground
black pepper

crusty bread or Plain, Buttery
Couscous (see page 103), to serve

Serves 4–6

For this lovely tagine, flavoured with garlic, chilli/chile, cumin and coriander/cilantro, you can use any meaty white fish. Serve it as a meal in itself with chunks of fresh, crusty bread to mop up the delicious juices, or with Plain, Buttery Couscous.

First, make the chermoula. Reserve 2 teaspoons of the mixture for cooking. Toss the fish chunks in the remaining chermoula, cover and leave to marinate in the refrigerator for 1–2 hours.

Meanwhile, bring a saucepan of water to the boil and add the potatoes. Boil vigorously for about 8 minutes to soften them a little, then drain and refresh under cold running water. Peel and cut in half lengthways.

Heat 2 tablespoons of the olive oil with the butter in a tagine or heavy-based saucepan. Stir in the garlic and, when it begins to brown, add the tomatoes to soften them. Add the skinned peppers and the reserved chermoula, and season to taste with salt and pepper. Tip the mixture onto a plate.

Arrange the potatoes over the base of the tagine and spoon half of the tomato and pepper mixture over them. Place the chunks of marinated fish on top and spoon the rest of the tomato and pepper mixture over the fish. Tuck the olives in and around the fish and drizzle the remaining tablespoon of olive oil over the top. Pour in 125 ml/½ cup of water, cover with a lid and steam for 15–20 minutes, until the fish is cooked through. Serve immediately with wedges of lemon and crusty bread or Plain, Butttery Couscous.

1 kg/2 lbs. 4 oz. boneless, skinless fish fillets such as cod or haddock, cut into large chunks

1 onion, coarsely chopped

a handful of fresh parsley leaves

2 garlic cloves, crushed

1 x 400-g/14-oz. can chopped tomatoes

4 thin carrots, halved and sliced

1 teaspoon ground cumin

½ teaspoon cayenne pepper

a pinch of sugar

sea salt and freshly ground black pepper

TO SERVE:

coriander/cilantro sprigs

lemon wedges

FOR THE MARINADE:

2 tablespoons chopped fresh coriander/cilantro leaves

1 tablespoon coarse sea salt

4 garlic cloves, crushed

2 tablespoons paprika

½ teaspoon cayenne pepper

1 tablespoon ground cumin

freshly squeezed juice of ½ a lemon

125 ml/½ cup olive oil

Serves 4

This recipe uses an ordinary baking dish, with foil in place of the conical tagine lid. Not authentic, but an acceptable replacement. Another slight modification is the use of fish fillets because it is more traditional to use whole fish. But the herbs and spices are based on a traditional Moroccan recipe and the taste is fabulously genuine.

Moroccan fish tagine

To make the marinade, combine the coriander/cilantro, salt, garlic, paprika, cayenne, cumin, lemon juice and olive oil in a shallow baking dish large enough to hold the fish in a single layer. Mix well. Add the fish, and use your hands to turn the pieces until they are coated in the oil. Cover with clingfilm/plastic wrap and refrigerate for at least 30 minutes.

Preheat the oven to 190°C (375°F) Gas 5.

To make the sauce, put the onion, parsley and garlic in a food processor and process until finely chopped. Transfer to a saucepan set over medium heat. Add the tomatoes, 300 ml/1¼ cups water, carrots, cumin, cayenne and sugar. Season, and stir to blend. Bring to the boil, then reduce the heat and simmer, covered, for about 15 minutes, until the carrots are tender.

Remove the fish from the refrigerator. Transfer it to a plate and pour the tomato sauce into the baking dish containing the marinade and mix well. Return the fish to the dish, arranging it on top of the sauce. Cover with kitchen foil and bake in the preheated oven for 10–20 minutes, until the fish is cooked through.

Remove from the oven, sprinkle with the coriander/cilantro sprigs and grind over some black pepper. Serve with the lemon wedges on the side for squeezing and Plain, Buttery Couscous or rice, as preferred.

oven-baked tagine of red mullet, tomatoes and lime

2 tablespoons olive oil

25 g/2 tablespoons butter

2–3 garlic cloves, thinly sliced

3–4 good-sized red mullet, gutted and cleaned

sea salt

2–3 large tomatoes, thinly sliced

1 lime, thinly sliced

TO SERVE:

leaves from a small bunch of fresh flat leaf parsley, coarsely chopped

1 lime, cut into wedges

Serves 3–4

Baking whole fish in a tagine keeps the flesh deliciously moist. Obviously, you need to select fish that fits snugly into your tagine or ovenproof dish. The most popular fish for oven-baking in North Africa include red mullet, sardines, red snapper, grouper and sea bass.

Preheat the oven to 180°C (350°F) Gas 4.

Heat the olive oil and butter in a tagine or large frying pan. Add the garlic and sauté, stirring, until it begins to brown. Put the fish in the tagine and cook it until the skin has browned and lightly buckled. (If you don't have a tagine, transfer the garlic and fish to an ovenproof dish at this stage.)

Turn off the heat, sprinkle a little salt over the fish and tuck the slices of tomato and lime over and around them. Cover and cook in the preheated oven for about 15 minutes.

Uncover and bake for a further 5–10 minutes, until the fish is cooked and nicely browned on top.

Sprinkle the parsley over the top and serve with wedges of lime to squeeze over the fish.

seafood tagine with saffron, ginger and fennel

4–5 tablespoons olive oil

20 raw king prawns/shrimp, with heads removed

2 onions, finely chopped

2 garlic cloves, finely chopped

5 cm/2 inches fresh ginger, peeled and finely chopped

a pinch of saffron threads

1–2 teaspoons smoked paprika

1 x 400-g/14-oz. can tomatoes, drained of juice

leaves from a small bunch of fresh coriander/cilantro, finely chopped

leaves from a small bunch of fresh flat leaf parsley, finely chopped

1 teaspoon sugar

4 fennel bulbs, trimmed and sliced thickly lengthways

sea salt and freshly ground black pepper

crusty bread, to serve

Serves 4

Many shellfish tagines are not so much traditional as they are inspired by cultural influences, such as the prawn/shrimp and mussel tagines of Tangier that resemble the cooking of Andalusia across the water. Serve this delicious tagine as a first or second course with chunks of crusty bread.

Heat 2–3 tablespoons of the olive oil in the base of a tagine or heavy-based casserole dish. Add the prawns/shrimp and cook for 2–3 minutes, until they turn opaque. Using a slotted spoon, remove the prawns/shrimp from the tagine and set aside. Keep the oil in the pan.

Stir the onion, garlic, ginger and saffron into the oil and sauté for 3–4 minutes, until they begin to colour. Add the paprika, tomatoes and half the herbs. Stir in the sugar and season with salt and pepper. Cook gently, partially covered, for about 10 minutes until the mixture thickens to form a sauce.

Meanwhile, steam the fennel for about 5 minutes, until it softens. Heat the remaining olive oil in a frying pan and add the steamed fennel. Cook gently on both sides for 4–5 minutes, until it turns golden. Sprinkle with salt and pepper.

Toss the cooked prawns/shrimp in the tomato sauce, place the fennel on top, cover, and cook gently for 5 minutes. Sprinkle with the remaining coriander/cilantro and parsley immediately before serving with crusty bread.

500 g/1 lb. 2 oz. fresh mussels in their shells, scrubbed and rinsed

500 g/1 lb. 2 oz. fresh prawns/shrimp in their shells, rinsed

freshly squeezed juice of 1 lemon

2 tablespoons olive oil

4–6 shallots, finely chopped

1 fennel bulb, chopped

1–2 teaspoons harissa paste (see page 17)

150 ml/⅓ cup double/heavy cream

leaves from a large bunch of fresh coriander/cilantro, finely chopped

sea salt and freshly ground black pepper

crusty bread, to serve

Serves 4–6

creamy shellfish tagine with fennel and harissa

In some coastal areas of Morocco, such as Casablanca and Tangier, restaurants offer shellfish tagines – a modern speciality, rather than a traditional one. This recipe is delicious served with chunks of crusty bread to mop up the creamy sauce.

Put the mussels and prawns/shrimp in a large saucepan with just enough water to cover them. Add the lemon juice, cover the pan and bring the liquid to the boil. Shake the pan and cook the shellfish for about 3 minutes, until the shells of the mussels have opened. Drain the shellfish, reserve the liquor, and discard any mussels that have not opened. Refresh the mussels and prawns/shrimp under cold running water and shell most of them (you can, of course, leave them all in their shells if you prefer, as long as you are prepared for messy eating).

Heat the olive oil in a tagine or heavy-based casserole dish. Add the shallots and fennel and sauté, stirring, until soft. Stir in the harissa and pour in 300 ml/1⅓ cup of the reserved cooking liquor. Bring the liquid to the boil and continue to boil for 2–3 minutes, reduce the heat and stir in the cream. Simmer gently for about 5 minutes to let the flavours mingle, season to taste with salt and pepper, and stir in the mussels and prawns/shrimp. Toss in half the coriander/cilantro, cover and cook gently for about 5 minutes. Sprinkle the remaining coriander/cilantro over the top and serve immediately with crusty bread.

VEGETABLE
TAGINES

tagine of butternut squash, shallots, sultanas and almonds

3 tablespoons olive oil plus
1 tablespoon butter

12 shallots, peeled and left whole

8 garlic cloves, lightly crushed

120 g/scant 1 cup sultanas/golden
raisins

120 g/scant 1 cup blanched
almonds

1–2 teaspoons harissa paste
(see page 17)

2 tablespoons dark, clear honey

1 medium butternut squash,
halved lengthways, peeled,
dcseeded and sliced

sea salt and freshly ground
black pepper

leaves from a small bunch of fresh
coriander/cilantro, finely chopped

TO SERVE:

lemon wedges

Plain, Buttery Couscous
(see page 103)

Serves 3–4

Substantial enough for a main meal, served with Plain, Buttery Couscous and yogurt, vegetable tagines also make good side dishes for grilled or roasted meats or other tagines. You can cook this recipe in the oven if you like, using the tagine base or an ovenproof dish.

Heat the oil and butter in a tagine or heavy-based casserole dish. Add the shallots and garlic and sauté, stirring, until they begin to colour. Add the sultanas/golden raisins and almonds and stir in the harissa paste and honey. Toss in the squash, making sure it is coated in the spicy oil. Pour in enough water to cover the base of the tagine and cover. Cook gently for 15–20 minutes, until the shallots and squash are tender but still quite firm.

Season to taste with salt and pepper, sprinkle the coriander/cilantro leaves over the top and serve with wedges of lemon to squeeze over the dish and Plain, Buttery Couscous, if liked.

2–3 tablespoons olive oil

2 red onions, halved and sliced

4 garlic cloves, crushed

2 teaspoons coriander seeds

1 teaspoon cumin seeds

2 teaspoons ground turmeric

1–2 teaspoons dried mint

8 medium waxy potatoes, peeled and quartered

350 ml/1⅔ cup vegetable or chicken stock

4 prepared artichokes, quartered

leaves from a small bunch of fresh coriander/cilantro, chopped

225 g/1½ cups shelled fresh peas or frozen peas

½ preserved lemon (see page 13), finely shredded

sea salt and freshly ground black pepper

TO SERVE:

leaves from a small bunch of fresh mint

crusty bread or Plain, Buttery Couscous (see page 103)

Serves 4–6

tagine of artichokes, potatoes and peas

You can make this hearty country dish with either fresh or frozen artichokes. If using fresh, you must first remove the outer leaves, then cut off the stems and scoop out the choke and hairy bits with a teaspoon. Rub the artichokes with lemon juice or place in a bowl of cold water with lemon juice to prevent discoloration.

Heat the olive oil in a tagine or heavy-based casserole dish. Add the onion and sauté, stirring, until it begins to soften. Add the garlic, coriander and cumin seeds, ground turmeric and the dried mint. Toss in the potatoes, coating them in the spices. Pour in the stock and bring to the boil. Reduce the heat, cover and cook gently for about 10 minutes.

Toss in the artichokes and fresh coriander/cilantro and cook for a further 5 minutes. Stir in the peas and preserved lemon, and season to taste with salt and pepper. Cook gently for 5–10 minutes, uncovered, until the artichokes are tender and the liquid has reduced.

Sprinkle with the fresh mint leaves and serve with crusty bread or Plain, Buttery Couscous.

2–3 tablespoons olive oil plus 1 tablespoon butter

7½ cm/3 inches fresh ginger, peeled and finely chopped or grated

1–2 cinnamon sticks or 1–2 teaspoons ground cinnamon

16 small shallots, peeled and left whole

700 g/1¾ lbs yam, peeled and cut into bite-sized pieces

2 medium carrots, peeled and cut into bite-sized pieces

175 g/¾ cup ready-to-eat pitted prunes

1 tablespoon dark, clear honey

425 ml/1¾ cups vegetable or chicken stock

leaves from a small bunch of fresh coriander/cilantro, roughly chopped

a few fresh mint leaves, chopped

sea salt and freshly ground black pepper

Plain, Buttery Couscous, to serve (see page 103)

Serves 4–6

tagine of yam, shallots, carrots and prunes

This syrupy, caramelized tagine is delicious served as a main dish, with Plain, Buttery Couscous and a herby salad, or as a side dish to accompany grilled or roasted meats. Sweet potatoes, butternut squash or pumpkin can be used instead of yam, if you prefer.

Heat the olive oil and butter in a tagine or heavy-based casserole dish. Add the ginger and cinnamon sticks. Toss in the shallots and when they begin to colour add the yam and the carrots. Sauté for 2–3 minutes, stirring, then add the prunes and the honey. Pour in the stock and bring it to the boil. Reduce the heat, cover and cook gently for about 25 minutes.

Uncover and stir in some of the coriander/cilantro and mint. Season to taste with salt and pepper and reduce the liquid, if necessary, by cooking for a further 2–3 minutes uncovered. The vegetables should be tender and slightly caramelized in a very syrupy sauce. Sprinkle with the remaining coriander/cilantro and mint and serve immediately with plain, buttery couscous, if liked.

tagine of beans, cherry tomatoes and black olives

175 g/ dried butter/lima beans, soaked in plenty of water for at least 6 hours

2–3 tablespoons olive oil plus 1 tablespoon butter

4 garlic cloves, halved and crushed

2 red onions, halved and sliced

1–2 fresh red or green chillies/chiles, thinly sliced

1–2 teaspoons coriander seeds, crushed

5 cm/2 inches fresh ginger, peeled and finely shredded or chopped

a pinch of saffron threads

16–20 cherry tomatoes

1–2 teaspoons sugar

1–2 teaspoons dried thyme

2–3 tablespoons black olives, pitted

freshly squeezed juice of 1 lemon

leaves from a small bunch of flat leaf parsley, coarsely chopped

sea salt and freshly ground black pepper

crusty bread and plain yogurt, to serve (optional)

Serves 4–6

As butter/lima beans are so meaty, this tagine makes a substantial main dish, but it is also excellent as an accompaniment to grilled or roasted meats and poultry. Bean dishes like this vary from region to region in Morocco, sometimes spiked with chillies/chiles or hot merguez, chorizo-style sausages.

Drain and rinse the soaked beans. Put them in a deep saucepan with plenty of water and bring to the boil. Boil for about 5 minutes, then reduce the heat and simmer gently for about 1 hour, or until the beans are tender but not mushy. Drain and refresh under cold running water.

Heat the olive oil and butter in a tagine or heavy-based casserole dish. Add the garlic, onions and chillies/chiles and sauté, stirring, until they soften. Add the coriander seeds, ginger and saffron. Cover and cook gently for 4–5 minutes. Toss in the tomatoes with the sugar and thyme, cover with the lid again, and cook until the skin on the tomatoes begins to crinkle.

Toss in the beans and olives, pour over the lemon juice and season to taste with salt and pepper. Cover and cook gently for about 5 minutes, until the beans and olives are heated through. Sprinkle with the flat leaf parsley and serve with crusty bread and a dollop of thick, creamy plain yogurt, if liked.

1–2 tablespoons olive oil

1 tablespoon butter or ghee

1–2 red onions, halved and sliced

3–4 garlic cloves, crushed

1–2 fresh red chillies/chiles, sliced

1–2 teaspoons coriander seeds, roasted and crushed

1–2 teaspoons cumin seeds, roasted and crushed

2 teaspoons sugar

16 baby aubergines/eggplant, with stalks intact

2 x 400-g/14-oz. cans chopped tomatoes

leaves from a bunch of fresh mint, roughly chopped

leaves from a bunch of fresh coriander/cilantro, roughly chopped

sea salt and freshly ground black pepper

Plain, Buttery Couscous (see page 103) and plain yogurt, to serve (optional)

Serves 4

This vegetarian tagine is best made with baby aubergines/eggplant, but you can also use larger aubergines/eggplant cut into quarters lengthways. As a main dish, it is delicious served with Plain, Buttery Couscous and a dollop of thick, creamy yogurt; it can also be served as a side dish to accompany meat or poultry.

tagine of baby aubergines with fresh herbs

Heat the oil and butter in a tagine or heavy-based casserole dish. Add the onions and garlic and sauté, stirring, until they begin to colour. Add the chillies/chiles, the coriander and cumin seeds and the sugar. When the seeds give off a nutty aroma, toss in the whole baby aubergines/eggplant, coating them in the onion and spices. Tip in the tomatoes, cover and cook gently for about 40 minutes, until the aubergines/eggplant are beautifully tender.

Season to taste with salt and pepper and add half the mint and coriander/cilantro leaves. Cover and simmer for a further 5–10 minutes. Sprinkle with the remaining mint and coriander/cilantro leaves and serve with Plain, Buttery Couscous and a dollop of thick, creamy plain yogurt, if liked.

spicy carrot and chickpea tagine with turmeric

3–4 tablespoons olive oil

1 onion, finely chopped

3–4 garlic cloves, finely chopped

2 teaspoons ground turmeric

1–2 teaspoons cumin seeds

1 teaspoon ground cinnamon

½ teaspoon cayenne pepper

½ teaspoon ground black pepper

1 tablespoon dark, clear honey

3–4 medium carrots, sliced on the diagonal

2 x 400-g/14-oz. cans chickpeas, rinsed and drained

sea salt

TO SERVE:

1–2 tablespoons rosewater

leaves from a bunch of fresh coriander/cilantro, finely chopped

lemon wedges

crusty bread and plain yogurt (optional)

Serves 4

This country-style dish is vegetarian, typical of regions where meat is regarded as a luxury by most families. Legumes of all kinds and, in particular, chickpeas, provide the nourishing content of these dishes. To avoid lengthy preparation and cooking, use canned chickpeas. For simple accompaniments, serve with lemon wedges, plain yogurt and crusty bread.

Heat the oil in a tagine or heavy-based casserole dish. Add the onion and garlic and sauté, stirring, until soft. Add the turmeric, cumin seeds, cinnamon, cayenne pepper, black pepper, honey and carrots. Pour in enough water to cover the base of the tagine and cover. Cook gently for about 10–15 minutes.

Toss in the chickpeas and check that there is still enough liquid at the base of the tagine, adding a little more water if necessary. Cover and cook gently for 5–10 minutes until the vegetables are tender.

Season with salt, sprinkle the rosewater and coriander/cilantro over the top and arrange the lemon wedges on the side. Serve with crusty bread and a dollop of thick, creamy plain yogurt, if liked.

baked vegetable tagine with preserved lemon

2–3 tablespoons olive oil

2 onions, halved and sliced

4 garlic cloves, chopped

5 cm/2 inches fresh ginger, peeled and chopped

1–2 fresh red chillies/chiles, chopped

1 teaspoon cumin seeds

1 teaspoon paprika

3–4 good-sized potatoes, peeled and thickly sliced

2 good-sized carrots, peeled and thickly sliced

8–10 broccoli florets

600 ml/2⅓ cups vegetable or chicken stock

225 g/1½ cups fresh or frozen peas

1 preserved lemon (see page 13), thickly sliced

leaves from a bunch of fresh coriander/cilantro, coarsely chopped

4–6 large tomatoes, sliced

15 g/1 tablespoon butter

sea salt and freshly ground black pepper

crusty bread or Plain, Buttery Couscous (see page 103), to serve

Serves 4

This vegetable tagine can be served as a side dish or on its own with Plain, Buttery Couscous or flat bread to dip into it. Vegetable tagines vary with the seasons and can be prepared on the stove or in the oven. For the baked version, you need a traditional Berber tagine with a domed lid, rather than the steep conical one, or you can use an ovenproof baking dish covered with foil.

Preheat the oven to 180ºC (350ºF) Gas 4.

Heat the oil in a tagine or heavy-based casserole dish. Add the onions and sauté until they begin to colour. Add the garlic, ginger and chillies/chiles and cook for 1–2 minutes. Stir in the cumin seeds and paprika then toss in the potatoes, carrots and broccoli. Pour in the stock, cover and place the tagine in the oven for about 20 minutes, until the potatoes, carrots and broccoli are tender but still firm and most of the liquid has reduced.

Season with salt and pepper. Toss in the peas, preserved lemon and half the coriander/cilantro. Arrange the tomato slices, overlapping each other, on top and dab them with little bits of butter. Put the tagine back into the oven, uncovered, to brown the tops of the tomatoes.

Garnish with the remaining coriander/cilantro and serve hot from the tagine with Plain, Buttery Couscous or crusty bread.

2 tablespoons olive oil or ghee

1 onion, halved lengthways
and sliced

2–3 garlic cloves, chopped

1–2 teaspoons coriander seeds

1 teaspoon cumin seeds

3 bell peppers (green, red and
yellow), sliced

2 tablespoons green olives,
pitted and finely sliced

4–6 eggs

1 teaspoon paprika or dried
chilli/hot pepper flakes

leaves from a small bunch of
flat leaf parsley, coarsely chopped

sea salt and freshly ground
black pepper

warmed flat breads, to serve

Serves 4–6

three-pepper tagine
with eggs

*This is one of those dishes you'll find in Morocco at street stalls,
bus stations and working men's cafes. Quick, easy and colourful,
it is a great dish for lunch or a tasty snack, served with warmed
flat breads.*

Heat the oil in the base of a tagine or heavy-based-casserole dish. Add
the onion, garlic, coriander and cumin seeds and sauté, stirring, until
the onions begin to soften. Toss in the peppers and olives and sauté
until they begin to colour. Season well with salt and pepper.

Using your spoon, push aside the peppers to form little pockets for the
eggs. Crack the eggs in the pockets and cover for 4–5 minutes until the
eggs are cooked. Scatter the paprika over the top and sprinkle with the
parsley. Serve immediately with warmed flat breads on the side.

COUSCOUS
DISHES

plain, buttery couscous

Traditionally, plain, buttery couscous, piled high in a mound, is served as a dish on its own after a tagine or roasted meat. It is held in such high esteem that religious feasts and celebratory meals would be unthinkable with it. The par-boiled couscous available outside Morocco is extremely easy to prepare, making it a practical accompaniment for many dishes featured in this book.

350 g/2 cups couscous, rinsed and drained

½ teaspoon sea salt

400 ml/1⅔ cup warm water

2 tablespoons olive or sunflower oil

25 g/2 tablespoons butter, broken into small pieces

TO SERVE:

15 g/1 tablespoon butter

2–3 tablespoons blanched, flaked almonds

Serves 4–6

Preheat the oven to 180°C (350°F) Gas 4.

Tip the couscous into an ovenproof dish. Stir the salt into the water and pour it over the couscous. Leave the couscous to absorb the water for about 10 minutes.

Using your fingers, rub the oil into the couscous grains to break up the lumps and aerate them. Scatter the butter over the surface and cover with a piece of foil or wet parchment paper. Put in the preheated oven for about 15 minutes, until the couscous is heated through.

Meanwhile, prepare the almonds. Melt the butter in a heavy-based frying pan set over medium heat, add the almonds and cook, stirring until they begin to turn golden. Remove from the pan and drain on kitchen paper.

Take the couscous out of the oven and fluff up the grains with a fork. Serve it from the dish or tip it onto a plate and pile it high in a mound, with the toasted almonds scattered over the top.

green couscous with a spring broth

This is a lovely fresh-tasting couscous dish, as it is prepared with delicious green vegetables, such as broad/fava beans and peas, artichokes, spring onions/scallions and baby courgettes/zucchini.

500 g/scant 3 cups couscous

½ teaspoon sea salt

600 ml/2⅓ cups warm water

1–2 tablespoons olive oil plus 1 tablespoon butter, broken into small pieces

1 litre/4 cups vegetable or chicken stock

350 g/2 cups fresh or frozen broad/fava beans, shelled

200 g/1¼ cups fresh or frozen peas

12 spring onions/scallions, sliced

6 baby courgettes/zucchini, sliced

4–6 artichoke hearts, quartered

leaves from a bunch of fresh flat leaf parsley, finely chopped

leaves from a bunch of fresh coriander/cilantro, finely chopped

leaves from a bunch of fresh mint, finely chopped

sea salt and freshly ground black pepper

Serves 4–6

Preheat the oven to 200°C (400°F) Gas 6.

Tip the couscous into an ovenproof dish. Stir the salt into the water and pour it over the couscous. Leave the couscous to absorb the water for about 10 minutes.

Using your fingers, rub the oil into the couscous grains to break up the lumps and aerate them. Scatter the butter over the surface and cover with a piece of foil or wet parchment paper. Put in the preheated oven for about 15 minutes, until the couscous is heated through.

Meanwhile, prepare the vegetable broth. Pour the stock into a heavy-based saucepan and bring it to the boil. Add the broad/fava beans, peas, spring onions/scallions, courgettes/zucchini and artichokes and cook for 5–10 minutes, until tender. Season the broth to taste with salt and pepper and stir in the herbs.

Remove the couscous from the oven and tip it onto a serving plate. Using a slotted spoon, lift the vegetables out of the broth and arrange them around, or over, the mound of couscous. Moisten with a little of the broth, then pour the rest into a jug and serve separately to pour over the couscous. Serve immediately.

8 baby aubergines/eggplant, left whole

3–4 small courgettes/zucchini, cut into 4 lengthways

2 red bell peppers, cut into 4 lengthways

4 garlic cloves, peeled and cut into 4 lengthways

5 cm/2 inches fresh ginger, peeled and cut into thin sticks

100 ml/scant ½ cup olive oil

leaves from a bunch of fresh coriander/cilantro, coarsely chopped

leaves from a bunch of fresh mint, coarsely chopped

sea salt

FOR THE LEMON COUSCOUS:

500 g/scant 3 cups couscous

½ teaspoon sea salt

600 ml/2⅓ cups warm water

1–2 tablespoons olive oil

1 preserved lemon (see page 13), finely chopped

15 g/1 tablespoon butter, broken into small pieces

Serves 4

This is a modern recipe and ideal for vegetarians. It is delicious on its own or served as an accompaniment to a meat or vegetable tagine. Generally, aubergines/eggplant, courgettes/zucchini and bell peppers are roasted together but you can vary the vegetables here according to the season.

lemon couscous with roasted vegetables

Preheat the oven to 200°C (400°F) Gas 6.

Put the vegetables, garlic and ginger in an ovenproof dish. Pour over the oil, sprinkle with salt and cook in the preheated oven for about 40 minutes, until the vegetables are tender and nicely browned.

To make the lemon couscous, tip the couscous into an ovenproof dish. Stir the salt into the water and pour it over the couscous. Leave it to absorb the water for about 10 minutes.

Using your fingers, rub the oil into the couscous grains to break up the lumps and aerate them. Toss in the preserved lemon, scatter the butter over the surface and cover with a piece of foil or wet parchment paper. Put the dish in the oven for about 15 minutes, until the couscous has heated through.

Tip the couscous onto a serving plate in a mound. Arrange the vegetables over and around it and spoon some of the roasting oil over the top. Sprinkle with the coriander/cilantro and mint and serve immediately.

350 g/2 cups couscous, rinsed and drained

400 ml/1⅔ cups warm water

2 tablespoons olive oil

2 teaspoons cumin seeds

2 teaspoons coriander seeds

2 teaspoons ground turmeric

1 tablespoon harissa paste (see page 17)

leaves from a small bunch of flat leaf parsley, finely chopped

2 litres/8 cups fish stock or water

4–6 garlic cloves, finely sliced

2 x 400-g/14-oz. cans plum tomatoes, drained of juice

2–3 carrots, cut into matchsticks

2–3 courgettes/zucchini, cut into matchsticks

2 tablespoons olive or sunflower oil

2 tablespoons butter, broken into small pieces

1 kg/2 lbs. 4 oz. firm-fleshed fish fillets

450 g/1 lb. uncooked prawns/shrimp, shelled and deveined

450 g/1 lb. fresh mussels, cleaned

450 g/1 lb. scallops, shelled and cleaned

leaves from a small bunch of fresh coriander/cilantro, finely chopped

sea salt and freshly ground black pepper

Serves 4–6

fish and shellfish k'dra with couscous

In the coastal regions, this is the king of fish dishes. Prepared in vast quantities for a family celebration, it combines the riches of the sea and the land in one big copper pot. Any firm-fleshed fish such as haddock, trout or sea bass will work here.

Preheat the oven to 180°C (350°F) Gas 4.

Tip the couscous grains into an ovenproof dish. Stir ½ teaspoon salt into the water and pour it over the couscous. Set aside for about 20 minutes.

Meanwhile, heat the oil in a large copper pot, or very large heavy-based saucepan. Stir in the cumin and coriander seeds, turmeric and harissa paste. Add the parsley and pour in the fish stock. Bring the liquid to the boil, reduce the heat and simmer for 5 minutes. Add the garlic, tomatoes, carrots and courgettes/zucchini and simmer for a further 10 minutes.

Using your fingers, rub the sunflower oil into the couscous grains to break up the lumps and aerate them. Scatter the butter over the top and cover with a piece of foil or wet greaseproof paper. Place in the oven for about 15 minutes to heat through.

Add the fish and shellfish to the simmering broth and cook for 5–10 minutes, until the fish is flaky, the prawns/shrimp opaque, and the shells of the mussels have opened (discard any that remain closed). Season to taste with salt and pepper and stir in the coriander/cilantro.

Fluff up the couscous with a fork and pile it onto a large serving plate in a domed mound. Spoon the fish and shellfish around the couscous and drizzle with a little of the broth. Ladle the rest of the broth into individual bowls and serve immediately.

couscous tfaia with beef

750 g/1 lb. 10 oz. beef rump or chuck, cut into bite-sized pieces

1 onion, chopped

1 teaspoon ground coriander

1 teaspoon ground cumin

a pinch of saffron strands

500 g/scant 3 cups couscous

500 ml/2 cups warm water

1–2 tablespoons olive oil

1 tablespoon butter, broken into small pieces

FOR THE TFAIA:

1–2 tablespoons olive oil plus 2 tablespoons butter

4 onions, thinly sliced

1–2 teaspoons cinnamon

1 teaspoon ground ginger

1 teaspoon saffron threads, soaked in 2 tablespoons warm water

2 tablespoons dark, clear honey

3 tablespoons sultanas/golden raisins, soaked in warm water for 15 minutes and drained

sea salt and freshly ground black pepper

Serves 4–6

This dish would traditionally be made in a couscoussière, a large pot with the meat cooking in the bottom compartment creating the steam for the couscous above. However, the couscous can be prepared separately and the dish combined at the end. The tfaia is a mixture of onions and sultanas/golden raisins that is spooned on top of the stew.

Preheat the oven to 180°C (350°F) Gas 4.

Put the beef in the base of a tagine or heavy-based casserole dish with the onion, spices and saffron. Pour in just enough water to cover, then bring to the boil. Reduce the heat, cover and simmer for about 1 hour.

Meanwhile, tip the couscous into an ovenproof dish. Stir ½ teaspoon salt into the water and pour it over the couscous. Leave the couscous to absorb the water for about 10 minutes. Using your fingers, rub the oil into the couscous grains to break up the lumps and aerate them. Scatter the butter over the top and cover with a piece of foil or wet parchment paper. Put the dish in the preheated oven for about 15 minutes, until the couscous is heated through.

To prepare the tfaia, heat the oil and butter in a heavy-based saucepan. Add the onions and sauté for 1–2 minutes, until softened. Reduce the heat and add the spices, saffron water and honey and season to taste with salt and pepper. Cover and cook gently for 15–20 minutes. Stir in the sultanas/golden raisins and cook, uncovered, for a further 10 minutes.

Tip the couscous onto a serving dish and create a well in the centre. Using a slotted spoon, transfer the meat into the well and top with the tfaia. Strain the cooking liquid from the meat and serve it separately as a sauce.

3 tablespoons olive oil

2 tablespoons butter

1 red onion, chopped

1 celery stalk, roughly chopped

6 garlic cloves, lightly smashed

500 ml/2 cups passata (Italian sieved tomatoes)

500 ml/2 cups vegetable stock

2 tablespoons fresh oregano leaves

1 parsnip, peeled and chopped

2 carrots, peeled and chopped

6 small, waxy, new potatoes

SPICED COUSCOUS:

375 ml/1½ cups vegetable stock

2 tablespoons butter

280 g/scant 2 cups medium grained couscous

1 teaspoon each of ground cumin, ground coriander and smoky Spanish paprika (pimentón)

¼ teaspoon cayenne pepper

Serves 4

root vegetable ragu with spiced couscous

This is a hearty dish packed with nutritious root vegetables. The method used for making the couscous in this recipe is not the traditional Moroccan way, but it does produce a full-flavoured version that makes a perfect accompaniment to the ragu.

Put the oil and butter in a large saucepan set over high heat. When the butter sizzles, add the onion, celery and garlic. Reduce heat to medium, partially cover the pan and cook for 10 minutes, stirring often, until the vegetables are soft and lightly browned. Add the passata, stock and oregano and bring to the boil. Reduce the heat to a medium simmer and cook, uncovered, for about 20 minutes. Add the parsnip, carrots and potatoes to the pan and cook for a further 15–20 minutes until tender.

To make the spiced couscous, put the stock and butter in a large saucepan set over high heat. Bring to the boil, then reduce the heat to low and keep the stock warm. Put the couscous and spices in a large, heavy-based saucepan and cook over medium/high heat until the spices are aromatic and just start to turn a dusky brown. Turn off the heat. Pour the warm stock into the pan. Stir, cover with a tight-fitting lid and let sit for 10 minutes. Fluff up the couscous with a fork, cover again and let sit for a further 5 minutes. Tip the couscous out into a bowl and fluff up to separate as many grains as possible. Serve immediately, topped with the root vegetable ragu.

SKEWERS, ROASTS
AND PAN FRIES

FOR THE SKEWERS:

500 g/1 lb. 2 oz. finely minced/ground lamb or beef

1 onion, finely chopped

2 garlic cloves, crushed

1–2 teaspoons ground cinnamon

1–2 teaspoons ras-el-hanout (see page 18)

1 teaspoon sea salt

leaves from a small bunch of fresh flat leaf parsley, finely chopped

leaves from a small bunch of fresh coriander/cilantro, finely chopped

FOR THE HARISSA COUSCOUS:

225 g/1⅓ cups couscous

225 ml/scant 1 cup warm water

½ teaspoon sea salt

1 tablespoon olive oil

2–3 teaspoons harissa paste (see page 17)

25 g/2 tablespoons butter, broken into small pieces

8–12 metal or wooden skewers

Serves 4–6

kefta skewers with harissa couscous

Another popular street dish throughout Morocco, these ground meat skewers vary from vendor to vendor, each with his own liberal pinch of spice or bunch of herbs. As the national spice ras-el-hanout is open to personal creation, the exact flavouring of some of these kefta skewers can be quite difficult to detect.

To make the skewers, mix the meat with the other ingredients and knead well, lifting the mixture up and slapping it back into the bowl to knock out the air, until it is smooth but slightly sticky. Cover and chill in the refrigerator for about 1–2 hours to allow the flavours to mingle.

Meanwhile, prepare the couscous. Tip the couscous into a large bowl. Stir the salt into the water and pour it over the couscous, stirring all the time so that the water is absorbed evenly. Leave the couscous to swell for about 10 minutes then, using your fingers, rub the oil and the harissa into the couscous.

Preheat the oven to 180°C (350°F) Gas 4 for the couscous and prepare the barbecue for the skewers. Divide the meat mixture into 8–12 portions and mould them into fat sausage shapes. Insert a skewer through each one.

Tip the couscous into an ovenproof dish, scatter the butter over the surface and cover with a piece of foil or wet parchment paper. Put the dish in the preheated oven for 15 minutes, until the couscous is heated through. Prepare the barbecue. Place the skewers on the barbecue and cook for 4–5 minutes on each side. Serve immediately.

souk skewers with roasted cumin and paprika

This is street food at its best. Quick, tasty and spicy, skewers like these are cooked by street vendors all over Morocco. The enticing aroma of charcoal-grilled meat and roasted cumin in the souks and medinas of Fes and Marrakesh wafts around every corner and through the labyrinthine streets. Also known by their French name, brochettes, these skewers are often served tucked into flat bread pouches with a dollop of tomato salsa or harissa paste.

1–2 onions, grated

2 teaspoons sea salt

450 g/1 lb. lean shoulder of lamb, trimmed and cut into bite-sized pieces

freshly squeezed juice of 1 lemon

2 teaspoons cumin seeds, roasted and ground

1–2 teaspoons paprika

leaves from a small bunch of fresh flat leaf parsley, finely chopped

leaves from a small bunch of fresh coriander/cilantro, finely chopped

freshly ground black pepper

1 lemon, cut into wedges, to serve

4 metal or wooden skewers

Serves 4

Put the grated onion in a bowl and sprinkle with the sea salt. Leave it to 'weep' for 10 minutes, then force it through a nylon sieve/strainer, or squeeze it with your hands, to extract the juice.

Put the lamb in a bowl and pour over the extracted onion juice. Add the lemon juice, roasted cumin, paprika, herbs and black pepper, to taste. Toss well so that the meat is thoroughly coated in the marinade. Cover and chill in the refrigerator for at least 2 hours, or overnight, to allow the flavours to penetrate the meat.

Prepare the barbecue. Thread the marinated meat onto skewers and put them on the barbecue. Cook for 3–4 minutes on each side until cooked through and serve immediately with wedges of lemon to squeeze over them.

16–20 chicken wings

4 oranges (blood oranges if available), cut into quarters

about 30 g/scant ½ cup icing/confectioners' sugar

½ a preserved lemon (see page 13), finely shredded or chopped

a small bunch of fresh coriander/cilantro, chopped

FOR THE MARINADE:

4 tablespoons harissa paste (see page 17)

2 tablespoons olive oil

sea salt

4 metal or wooden skewers

Serves 4

harissa chicken wings with oranges and preserved lemon

With all the flavours of Morocco, this recipe is quick and easy and best eaten with fingers. The oranges are there to suck on after an explosion of fire on the tongue. They can be cooked separately, or threaded alternately on metal skewers.

For the marinade, mix the harissa paste with the olive oil to form a loose paste and add a little salt. Brush the oily mixture over the chicken wings, so that they are well coated. Leave to marinate for 2 hours.

Thread the marinated chicken wings onto the skewers. Prepare the barbecue. Put the chicken on the barbecue and cook on both sides for about 5 minutes. Once the wings begin to cook, dip the orange quarters lightly in icing/confectioners' sugar, thread them onto skewers and cook for a few minutes, checking that they are slightly charred but not burnt.

Serve the chicken wings and oranges together and scatter the preserved lemon and coriander/cilantro over the top.

monkfish skewers with chermoula

1 quantity Chermoula (see page 28)

900 g/2 lbs. monkfish tail, cut into chunks

12–16 cherry tomatoes

TO SERVE:

1–2 teaspoons smoked paprika

leaves from a small bunch of fresh coriander/cilantro, chopped

1–2 lemons, halved

cooked rice

4–6 metal skewers or 4–6 wooden skewers, soaked in water before use

Serves 4–6

Chermoula is a classic Moroccan flavouring of garlic, chilli/chile, cumin and fresh coriander/cilantro, which is employed as a marinade for fish and chicken tagines and grilled dishes. Any meaty, white fish can be used for this recipe but monkfish cooks particularly well over charcoal.

First, make the chermoula. Place the fish in a shallow dish and rub with the chermoula. Cover and chill in the refrigerator for 1–2 hours.

Thread the marinated monkfish and cherry tomatoes alternately onto the skewers. Prepare the barbecue. Cook the skewers for about 2 minutes on each side, until the monkfish is nicely browned. Dust with a little paprika and sprinkle with coriander/cilantro and serve immediately with rice and lemon wedges for squeezing.

spicy pan-grilled aubergine with honey

8 aubergines/eggplant, thickly sliced lengthways

olive oil, for brushing

2–3 cloves garlic, crushed

5 cm/2 inches fresh ginger, peeled and crushed

1 teaspoon ground cumin

1 teaspoon harissa paste (see page 17)

5 tablespoons dark, clear honey

freshly squeezed juice of 1 lemon

leaves from a small bunch of fresh flat leaf parsley, finely chopped

sea salt

Plain, Buttery Couscous (see page 103), to serve

4 metal or wooden skewers, to serve (optional)

Serves 4

Hot, spicy, sweet and fruity are classic combinations in Moroccan cooking. This delicious dish is perfect served on its own with Plain, Buttery Couscous or to accompany grilled meat. You can cook the aubergines/eggplant in a ridged stove-top grill pan or under the grill/broiler.

Brush each aubergine/eggplant slice with olive oil and cook them in a stove-top grill pan or grill/broil them under a conventional grill/broiler, turning them over so that they are lightly browned.

In a wok or large heavy-based frying pan, fry the garlic in a little olive oil, then stir in the ginger, cumin, harissa paste, honey and lemon juice. Add a little water to thin it, then place the aubergine/eggplant slices in the liquid and cook gently for about 10 minutes, until they have absorbed the sauce. Add more water if necessary and season to taste with salt.

Thread the aubergines/eggplant onto the skewers, if using, and garnish with the parsley. Serve hot or at room temperature with Plain, Buttery Couscous.

a 2-kg/4-lb. 8 oz. leg of lamb

200 ml/scant 1 cup water

2–3 tablespoons dark, clear honey

10–12 pieces of fresh fruit, such as figs, plums or apricots (optional)

leaves from a bunch of fresh coriander/cilantro, roughly chopped

sea salt and freshly ground black pepper

FOR THE SMEN COATING:

4 garlic cloves, chopped

7.5 cm/3 inches fresh ginger, peeled and chopped

1 fresh red chilli/chile, chopped

a generous pinch of sea salt

a small bunch each of fresh coriander/cilantro and flat leaf parsley, chopped

1–2 teaspoons ground cumin

1–2 teaspoons ground coriander

3 tablespoons softened smen, butter or olive oil (see page 14)

Plain, Buttery Couscous (see page 103)

a handful of chopped almonds and pistachios (optional)

fresh figs, plums, apricots or quince, to serve (optional)

Serves 6

roasted smen-coated lamb with honey mechoui

Traditionally, this is a festive dish, as an entire lamb or kid is roasted slowly over embers over a pit dug in the ground and shared among a community or a large family. When cooking a joint of lamb in a communal oven, Moroccan cooks often add seasonal fruit, such as fresh figs, plums, apricots or quince to the dish.

First, make the smen coating. Using a mortar and pestle, pound the garlic, ginger and chilli/chile with enough salt to form a coarse paste. Add the fresh coriander/cilantro and parsley, pound to a paste and stir in the ground cumin and coriander. Put the smen in a bowl and beat in the paste until thoroughly mixed. Cut small incisions in the leg of lamb with a sharp knife and rub the spicy smen all over the meat, making sure it goes into the incisions. Cover and leave in the refrigerator for at least 2 hours.

Preheat the oven to 200°C (400°F) Gas 4. Transfer the leg of lamb to a roasting dish and pour the water around it. Roast in the preheated oven for about 1 hour 15 minutes, basting from time to time, until it is nicely browned. Spoon the honey over the lamb and place the fresh figs, plums or apricots around the meat, if using. Return the dish to the oven for a further 15 minutes.

Put the roasted lamb in a serving dish and leave it to rest for about 15 minutes before serving. Meanwhile, heat the juices in the roasting dish, season with salt and pepper, and pour over the roast lamb. Sprinkle the coriander/cilantro over the top and, if using fruit, arrange it around the dish. Serve accompanied by a mound of Plain, Buttery Couscous tossed with chopped almonds and pistachios.

roast chicken stuffed with couscous, apricots and dates

2 garlic cloves, crushed

2 teaspoons dried oregano

1–2 teaspoons paprika

2 tablespoons butter, softened

1 large organic chicken, about 1.5 kg/3 lbs. 5 oz.

1 sliced off orange end

150 ml/⅔ cup chicken stock

green salad, to serve

FOR THE COUSCOUS STUFFING:

225 g/1½ cups couscous

½ teaspoon salt

225 ml/scant 1 cup warm water

1 tablespoon olive oil

1–2 teaspoons ground cinnamon

1 teaspoon ground coriander

½ teaspoon ground cumin

1 tablespoon dark, clear honey

2 tablespoons golden raisins

125 g/½ cup ready-to-eat dried apricots, thickly sliced

125 g/½ cup ready-to-eat dates, thickly sliced or chopped

2–3 tablespoons blanched almonds, roasted

Serves 4–6

Throughout Morocco whole chickens are generally spit-roasted, grilled over charcoal or cooked in large tagines. Oven-roasting tends to be the method employed in the contemporary kitchens of the big towns and cities. Stuffed with aromatic, fruity couscous, this dish is really a meal on its own, accompanied by a salad.

Preheat the oven to 180°C (350°F) Gas 4. To make the stuffing, tip the couscous into a large bowl. Stir the salt into the warm water and pour it over the couscous, stirring all the time so that the water is absorbed evenly. Leave the couscous to swell for about 10 minutes then, using your fingers, rub the oil into the couscous to break up the lumps and aerate it. Stir in the other stuffing ingredients and set aside.

In a small bowl, beat the garlic, oregano and paprika into the softened butter then smear it all over the chicken, inside and out. Put the chicken in the base of a tagine or in an ovenproof dish and fill the cavity with as much of the couscous stuffing as you can (any left-over couscous can be heated through in the oven before serving and fluffed up with a little extra oil or butter). Seal the cavity with the slice of orange (you can squeeze the juice from the rest of the orange over the chicken). Pour the stock into the base of the tagine and roast the chicken in the oven for 1–1½ hours, basting from time to time, until the chicken is cooked.

Remove the chicken from the oven and allow it to rest for 10 minutes before carving or jointing it and strain the cooking juices into a jug. Heat up any remaining couscous (as described above) and serve this with the chicken, the jug of cooking juices to pour over and a green salad.

grilled sardine sandwiches stuffed with chermoula

1 quantity Chermoula
(see page 28)

8 large or 16 small fresh sardines, gutted and boned with heads removed (you can ask the fishmonger to do this for you)

1 egg, beaten

sea salt

1 lemon, cut into quarters, to serve

Serves 4

The classic Moroccan marinade for fish called chermoula varies from cook to cook but gives the dishes a very distinct taste. In this dish the sardines are boned and butterflied and sandwiched together with the chermoula filling. Extremely fresh and tasty, the sardines can be grilled or fried and are best enjoyed on their own with a little lemon to squeeze over them.

First, make the chermoula. Open out the sardines and place half of them skin-side down on a flat surface. Smear the chermoula over the sardines and brush the sides with beaten egg. Place the remaining butterflied sardines on top to sandwich the mixture together.

Prepare the barbecue. Put the sardines on the heated barbecue and cook for 2–3 minutes on each side. Sprinkle with salt and serve immediately with the lemon wedges for squeezing.

2–3 tablespoons plain/all-purpose flour

2–3 fresh snapper, skinned and cut into chunks

sunflower oil, for shallow frying

leaves from a small bunch of fresh flat leaf parsley, coarsely chopped

sea salt and freshly ground black pepper

1 lemon, cut into wedges, to serve

bread, to serve

FOR THE SAUCE:

2–3 tablespoons olive oil

1 onion, chopped

2 garlic cloves, chopped

1–2 teaspoons harissa paste (see page 17)

1 cinnamon stick

2 teaspoons sugar

1 x 400 g/14-oz. can of chopped tomatoes, drained of juice

2–3 tablespoons black or kalamata olives

Serves 4

In Morocco, fresh fish is often grilled or fried at stalls in the street and served with bread, or a little fiery sauce. You can use any firm-fleshed fish, such as snapper, sea bream, sea bass, monkfish or trout for this dish, which is delicious served on its own with chunks of bread to mop up the sauce.

pan-fried snapper with harissa and olive sauce

To make the sauce, heat the oil in a heavy-based saucepan. Stir in the onion and garlic and cook for 2–3 minutes, until they begin to colour. Stir in the harissa paste, cinnamon stick and sugar and add the tomatoes. Cook for 4–5 minutes then add the olives and season to taste with salt and pepper. Remove from the heat and cover to keep the sauce hot.

Season the flour with salt and pepper and toss the fish chunks in it. Heat the oil in a frying pan, add the fish chunks and fry them for about 2 minutes on each side, until golden brown. Drain the fish chunks on paper towels and transfer them to a serving dish. Spoon the sauce over and around the fish and sprinkle with parsley. Serve with bread and wedges of lemon for squeezing.

pan-fried seafood with ginger, cumin and paprika

3 tablespoons olive oil

2–3 garlic cloves, chopped

5 cm/2 inches fresh ginger, peeled and grated

1 fresh red chilli/chile, chopped

1 teaspoon cumin seeds

1 teaspoon paprika

500 g/1 lb. 2 oz. raw king prawns/shrimp, shells on

leaves from a bunch of fresh coriander/cilantro, finely chopped

sea salt and freshly ground black pepper

TO SERVE:

crusty bread

1 lemon, cut into wedges

Serves 4

This is a quick, easy way of preparing prawns/shrimp for a snack or a main meal. Simply serve the juicy, piquant prawns/shrimp from the cooking vessel with chunks of crusty bread to mop up the oil and spices left behind.

Heat the oil in the base of a tagine or a large, heavy-based frying pan. Stir in the garlic, ginger, chilli/chile and cumin seeds. As soon as a lovely aroma rises from the pan, add the paprika and toss in the prawns/shrimp. Fry quickly over medium heat, until the prawns/shrimp are just cooked and have turned opaque. Season to taste with salt and pepper and sprinkle with coriander/cilantro. Serve the prawns/shrimp immediately with crusty bread and lemon wedges for squeezing.

baked trout
stuffed with dates

4 small or 2 large fresh trout, gutted, rinsed and patted dry

3 tablespoons olive oil plus 1 tablespoon butter, or 2 tablespoons ghee

1 onion, finely chopped

5 cm/2 inches fresh ginger, peeled and finely chopped

2–3 teaspoons ground cinnamon plus 1 teaspoon for dusting

2–3 tablespoons blanched almonds, finely chopped

100 g/scant ½ cup medium- or short-grain rice, rinsed and drained

200 g/scant 1 cup moist, ready-to-eat dates, chopped

leaves from a small bunch of fresh coriander/cilantro, finely chopped

a small bunch of fresh flat leaf parsley, finely chopped

1 orange, cut into thin slices

sea salt and freshly ground black pepper

Serves 4

Cooking fish with dates is a lovely Moroccan tradition. Trout and shad are often selected for this dish, which can be cooked in a tagine on the stove or in the oven. Cooking fish in this manner is often reserved for banquets and family celebrations where the whole fish is displayed with dates stuffed with almond paste.

Preheat the oven to 180°C (350°F) Gas 4. Season the cavities of the fish with salt and pepper. Line an ovenproof dish with kitchen foil, so that the fish can be wrapped in it, and place the fish on the foil.

Heat most of the oil and butter or ghee in a heavy-based saucepan. Stir in the onion and ginger and cook for 2–3 minutes, until they begin to colour. Stir in the cinnamon and almonds, add the rice and season to taste with salt and pepper. Pour in just enough water to cover the rice and bring it to the boil. Reduce the heat and simmer gently until all the water has been absorbed. Turn off the heat, cover the pan and leave the rice to steam for 10 minutes.

Add the dates, coriander/cilantro and parsley to the rice and let it cool before stuffing the fish with it. To do this, spoon the filling into the cavities and brush the tops of the fish with the remaining oil or ghee. Place the orange slices around the fish, wrap up the foil to form a package, and place the dish in the preheated oven for 15–20 minutes. Open the foil and bake for a further 5 minutes, to lightly brown the top. Decorate the fish with a thin line of ground cinnamon by rubbing it between your thumb and index finger. Serve immediately.

char-grilled quails with kumquats

4 quails, cleaned and boned

2–3 tablespoons olive oil

freshly squeezed juice of 1 orange

5 cm/2 inches fresh ginger, peeled and grated

a pinch of saffron strands

225 g/8 oz. kumquats, halved

2 tablespoons dark, clear honey

1 teaspoon paprika

leaves from a bunch of fresh coriander/cilantro, roughly chopped

12 wooden skewers, soaked in water for 20 minutes or 12 metal skewers

Serves 4

This is great finger food, ideal for a barbecue. In Morocco, pigeons, quails and poussins are cooked this way and served straight from the grill with bread. As the quails in this recipe are boned, you can easily slip them into the pocket of a pita bread, or you can serve them with any crunchy Moroccan salad.

Thread a skewer through the wings of each quail and a second skewer through the thighs, so that each quail has 2 skewers through it. Put the quails in a shallow dish.

Mix the olive oil, orange juice, ginger and saffron together in a bowl and smear the mixture over the quails. Cover with clingfilm/plastic wrap and place in the refrigerator for 2–3 hours, turning the quails in the marinade from time to time.

Meanwhile, prepare the barbecue and thread the kumquats onto the remaining skewers. Place the quails on the barbecue, brushing them with any leftover marinade, and cook them for about 4 minutes on each side. Halfway through the cooking time, put the kumquats on the barbecue with the quails and cook them until they are slightly charred.

Remove the quails and kumquats from the barbecue and serve immediately, drizzled with honey and sprinkled with the paprika and chopped coriander/cilantro.

char-grilled harissa chicken

1–2 tablespoons harissa paste
(see page 17)

4 tablespoons olive oil

8–12 chicken drumsticks

a bunch of fresh
coriander/cilantro

sea salt

Serves 4

*Along with the ubiquitous lamb skewers, Moroccan street
vendors sell harissa-coated chicken legs and wings. Served
as part of a barbecue at home, the chicken legs can be
wrapped in paper or coriander/cilantro to hold, or served
with a salad on the side.*

Put the harissa paste in a bowl and stir in the olive oil until
blended. Season with salt and smear the mixture over the chicken.
Cover and chill in the refrigerator for about 2 hours.

Prepare the barbecue. Place the marinated drumsticks on the
barbecue and cook for about 4–5 minutes on each
side. Wrap them in coriander/cilantro, and
serve immediately.

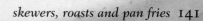

roast duck with honey, pears and figs

This is a delicious way to cook duck, or you could try it with lamb. Overall, the dish is very sweet, so you could alter the amount of honey and sugar to your taste. Serve the duck with Plain, Buttery Couscous.

5 cm/2 inches fresh ginger, peeled and chopped

2 garlic cloves, chopped

2–3 tablespoons olive oil

4 duck legs, skin on

2 pears, cored and cut into quarters

4 fresh figs, cut into quarters

2 teaspoons sugar

2 teaspoons ground cinnamon

1–2 tablespoons dark, clear honey

sea salt

TO SERVE:

2 teaspoons toasted sesame seeds

Plain, Buttery Couscous
(see page 103)

Serves 4

Using a mortar and pestle, pound the ginger with the garlic and a little salt to form a paste. Beat 2 tablespoons of the oil into the paste. Make incisions all over the duck legs using a sharp knife. Put the legs in a dish and rub the oil and ginger mixture all over them, making sure you get it into the incisions. Cover and chill in the refrigerator for at least 2 hours.

Preheat the oven to 200°C (400°F) Gas 6. Transfer the marinated duck legs to a rack in a roasting pan and roast them in the oven for about 30 minutes, until golden.

Remove the duck legs from the oven and drain off any excess fat. Tip 1 tablespoon of the duck fat into a heavy-based saucepan and stir in the pears and figs. Sprinkle the sugar and cinnamon over the fruit and cook for 2–3 minutes, until slightly caramelized.

Transfer the duck legs to the roasting pan and surround them with the pears and figs. Drizzle the honey over the duck and return it to the oven. Roast for a further 10 minutes, then serve immediately with Plain, Buttery Couscous andthe sesame seeds sprinkled over the top.

VEGETABLE
SIDE DISHES

baked aubergines

When they are in season, there is often an aubergine/eggplant dish on the table as part of a Moroccan meal. Versatile and filling, aubergines/eggplant are used in many ways, as side dishes, snacks, main meals and even desserts. This dish can be served as a course on its own or as a side dish to roasted and grilled meats.

2 aubergines/eggplant, halved lengthways

2–3 tablespoons olive oil, plus extra for drizzling

1 onion, chopped

2 tomatoes, skinned and chopped plus 1 tomato, skinned and thinly sliced

2 garlic cloves, crushed

50 g/1 cup fresh breadcrumbs, toasted

a small bunch of fresh coriander/cilantro, chopped

1–2 teaspoons harissa paste (see page 17)

1 teaspoon sugar

sea salt and freshly ground black pepper

Serves 4

Preheat the oven to 180°C (350°F) Gas 4. Using a spoon, scoop out the aubergine/eggplant flesh and place it on a chopping board. Brush the insides of the empty aubergine/eggplant shells with a little olive oil, place them on a baking sheet and bake them in the oven for 4–5 minutes.

Meanwhile, coarsely chop the aubergine/eggplant flesh. Heat the remaining oil in a pan and fry the onion to soften. Add the aubergine/ eggplant flesh, cook for a few minutes more then stir in the chopped tomatoes. Add the garlic, breadcrumbs, coriander/cilantro, harissa paste and sugar. Season to taste with salt and pepper.

Spoon the mixture into the empty aubergine/eggplant shells. Arrange the slices of tomato on the top of each one, drizzle with a little olive oil and bake in the preheated oven for 20–25 minutes. Serve hot.

150 g/scant 1 cup couscous

½ teaspoon salt

150 ml/⅔ cup warm water

3–4 tablespoons olive oil, plus extra for drizzling

4 large tomatoes

1 onion, finely chopped

1 carrot, peeled and diced

a sprinkling of sugar

1–2 teaspoons ras-el-hanout (see page 18)

a bunch each of fresh flat leaf parsley and fresh coriander/cilantro, finely chopped

½ preserved lemon, finely chopped (see page 13)

sea salt and freshly ground black pepper

Serves 4

Casablancan stuffed tomatoes

In season, there is such an abundance of sun-ripened tomatoes that they are used in salads, added to couscous, tagines, roasted, grilled or stuffed. In Casablanca, these tomatoes stuffed with couscous and herbs are popular as an appetizer, or they are served as a main meal with a salad.

Preheat the oven to 180°C (350°F) Gas 4. Put the couscous in a bowl. Stir the salt into the warm water and pour it over the couscous, stirring all the time so that the water is absorbed evenly. Leave the couscous to swell for about 10 minutes before using your fingers to rub 1 tablespoon of the oil into the couscous to break up the lumps and aerate them.

Slice the top off each tomato and set aside. Using a spoon, scoop out the pulp and seeds and reserve in a bowl. In a heavy-based saucepan, heat the remaining olive oil and stir in the onion and carrot. Fry until they begin to caramelize, then stir in the tomato pulp and sugar. Add the ras-el-hanout and cook until the mixture forms a thick sauce. Season to taste with salt and pepper.

Tip the spicy tomato mixture onto the couscous and mix well. Add the fresh herbs and preserved lemon and toss until it is thoroughly combined. Spoon the couscous into each tomato cavity and place a top on each one like a lid. Put the filled tomatoes in a baking dish, drizzle with a little olive oil and bake in the preheated oven for about 25 minutes. Serve hot or leave to cool and eat at room temperature as they are or with a salad on the side.

spicy potato omelette

This deliciously spicy omelette can be cut into thin strips and served as an appetizer, or divided into segments and presented as a snack or as a side dish with grilled food. The entire omelette can be cooked on the stove and browned under the grill/broiler, or it can be baked in the oven.

4–6 medium potatoes, unpeeled and halved

1 teaspoon sea salt

6–8 eggs

1 teaspoon ground turmeric

1 teaspoon ground cumin

1 teaspoon paprika

½ teaspoon ground coriander

a small bunch of fresh flat leaf parsley, finely chopped

1 tablespoon olive oil

sea salt and freshly ground black pepper

Serves 4–6

Put the potatoes in a saucepan with plenty of water and bring to the boil. Add the salt and boil the potatoes until soft enough to mash. Drain and refresh under cold running water. Peel off the skins, transfer the potatoes to a bowl and mash them. Beat the eggs into the potatoes and add the spices and parsley. Season to taste with salt and pepper.

Heat the oil in a heavy-based frying pan, then tip in the potato mixture, making sure it spreads evenly in the pan. Cover and cook over low heat for 10–15 minutes, until the omelette has puffed up and is firm to the touch. Place the pan under a preheated medium/hot grill/broiler for 3–4 minutes to brown the top of the omelette. Cut it into strips or segments to serve.

sautéed spinach with orange and almonds

500 g/6 cups fresh spinach leaves, thoroughly rinsed and drained

2–3 tablespoons olive oil plus 1 tablespoon butter

1 onion, roughly chopped

2 garlic cloves, finely chopped

freshly squeezed juice and rind of 1 orange

2 tablespoons flaked almonds, toasted

sea salt and freshly ground black pepper

Serves 2–4

This dish is generally made with spinach or mallow, which grows wild in the countryside and is picked for vegetable dishes and soup. Quite often you will come across makeshift stalls selling bunches of mallow by the dusty roadside.

Put the spinach in a steamer and cook for 8–10 minutes, until soft. Tip the cooked spinach onto a wooden board and chop to a pulp. Set aside. Heat the oil and butter in a heavy-based saucepan. Stir in the onion and garlic and cook until they begin to colour. Add the spinach and mix until thoroughly combined. Add the orange juice and rind and season to taste with salt and pepper. Tip the spinach into a serving dish and garnish with the toasted almonds.

braised vegetables with aniseed

3–4 tablespoons olive oil

2 fennel bulbs, trimmed and chopped

2 medium courgettes/zucchini, trimmed and cubed

1 tablespoon butter

2 teaspoons aniseeds

½ preserved lemon, very thinly sliced (see page 13)

sea salt and freshly ground black pepper

Serves 4

Braised vegetables, such as courgettes/zucchini and artichokes, are often combined with fruit or spices and served as an accompaniment to tagines or roasted meats. This recipe from Casablanca is light and aromatic rather than spicy and complements the varied fish tagines.

Heat the oil in a heavy-based frying pan and stir in the fennel. Cover with a lid and cook gently for 10–15 minutes. Stir in the courgettes/zucchini and cook for a further 5 minutes, until they begin to soften.

Add the butter and the aniseeds and toss thoroughly. Season to taste with salt and pepper, sprinkle with the preserved lemon and serve immediately.

honey-glazed pumpkin with spices

700 g/1 lb. 9 oz. pumpkin flesh, with skin and seeds removed

50 g/3½ tablespoons butter

2–3 tablespoons dark, clear honey

2 cinnamon sticks

3–4 cloves

1 teaspoon ground ginger

½ teaspoon cayenne

leaves from a small bunch of fresh coriander/cilantro, finely chopped

sea salt and freshly ground black pepper

Serves 4

Root vegetables and members of the squash family, such as sweet potatoes, turnips, butternut and pumpkins, are often cooked with honey and spices, as their sweet flesh remains succulent and marries well with the flavours. Generally, these side dishes are served with grilled or roasted meats.

Preheat the oven to 180°C (350°F) Gas 4. Put the pumpkin in a steamer and cook for about 10 minutes, until the flesh is tender but still firm. Tip the steamed flesh into an ovenproof dish.

Melt the butter in a saucepan and stir in the honey. Add the cinnamon sticks, cloves, ground ginger and cayenne and season to taste with salt and pepper. Pour the mixture over the pumpkin then bake in the preheated oven for 15–20 minutes.

Tip the glazed pumpkin onto a serving plate, remove the cinnamon and cloves, then sprinkle with the coriander/cilantro. Serve warm as a side dish to roasted or grilled chicken or meat.

4–5 tablespoons olive oil

1 onion, halved and sliced

2 garlic cloves, chopped

1 red bell pepper, halved and sliced

1 medium aubergine/eggplant, halved and sliced

2 courgettes/zucchini, sliced

225 g/1 cup pitted, ready-to-eat dates, halved lengthways

2 x 400-g/14-oz. cans chopped tomatoes

1–2 teaspoons sugar

2 teaspoons ras-el-hanout (see page 18)

a small bunch of fresh flat leaf parsley, coarsely chopped

sea salt and freshly ground black pepper

Serves 4–6

Moroccan ratatouille with dates

Similar to a French ratatouille, this delicious dish is spiked with a touch of ras-el-hanout and sweetened with succulent dates. It can be served with bread or couscous, or as an accompaniment to a tagine, grilled meats or fish.

Heat the oil in a tagine or a heavy-based casserole dish. Stir in the onion and garlic and cook for 2–3 minutes until they begin to soften. Add the pepper, aubergine/eggplant and courgettes/zucchini and cook for a further 3–4 minutes. Add the dates, tomatoes, sugar and Ras-el-hanout and mix thoroughly. Cover with a lid and cook for about 40 minutes, until the vegetables are tender.

Season to taste with salt and pepper. Sprinkle the chopped parsley over the top and serve hot.

aubergine slices in spiced honey

2 medium aubergines/eggplant

4 tablespoons olive oil

3 garlic cloves

5 cm/2 inches fresh ginger, finely grated

1½ teaspoons ground cumin

½ teaspoon cayenne pepper or hot chilli/chili powder

6 tablespoons dark, clear honey

freshly squeezed juice of 1 lemon

150 ml/⅔ cup water

chopped flat leaf parsley, to serve

sea salt

Serves 4

The sweetness of the honey combined with fresh ginger, garlic and a touch of spice from the cayenne pepper gives the aubergines/eggplant a delicious depth of flavour.

Preheat the grill/broiler to high. Cut the aubergines/eggplant into rounds about 1 cm/½ inch thick. Dip them in olive oil, turning them over, and sprinkle with salt. Cook under the hot grill/broiler, turning them over once, until they are lightly browned. Put the garlic and ginger in a large frying pan with the remaining oil and sauté for 1–2 minutes, until golden. Add the cumin, cayenne pepper, honey, lemon juice and water and cook for another 2 minutes. Add the aubergine/eggplant slices and cook over low heat for about 10 minutes, until they are soft. Sprinkle with the chopped parsley to serve.

roasted flat mushrooms with spiced squash stuffing

1 small squash (about 900 g/ 2 lbs.), peeled and diced

5–6 tablespoons olive oil

a small bunch of thyme

¼ teaspoon dried chilli/hot pepper flakes

1 garlic clove, chopped

1 x 400-g/14-oz. can chickpeas

½–1 teaspoon ground toasted cumin seeds

freshly squeezed lemon juice, to taste

1–2 tablespoons chopped flat leaf parsley

1–2 tablespoons crème fraîche/sour cream (optional)

8 large, flat portobello mushrooms, stalks removed

4 tablespoons toasted pumpkin seeds

sea salt and freshly ground black pepper

FOR THE SAUCE:

1 garlic clove

a pinch of coarse sea salt

3–4 tablespoons tahini

freshly squeezed lemon juice, to taste

4–5 tablespoons plain yogurt

1 tablespoon chopped mint

Serves 4

This is good enough to serve as a meat-free appetizer or as a main dish when entertaining friends, with a rice pilaf and maybe a spinach salad. It also makes a delicious family supper dish, as it is full of warm, comforting flavours.

Preheat the oven to 220°C (425°F) Gas 7. Toss the squash with 3 tablespoons of the oil, 1 teaspoon chopped thyme, the chilli/hot pepper flakes and garlic. Season and put on a baking sheet. Cover with kitchen foil and cook in the preheated oven for about 30 minutes until tender, then uncover and cook for a further 10 minutes. Let cool and put in a food processor with the chickpeas. Whizz to make a rough purée. Season to taste with salt, pepper, cumin and lemon juice, then stir in the parsley. If the purée is very dry, add the crème fraîche/sour cream or a little water.

Meanwhile, put the mushrooms, gill-side uppermost, on an oiled baking sheet. Season and sprinkle with a few thyme leaves. Drizzle with the remaining oil and a good squeeze of lemon juice. Roast, uncovered, in the preheated oven for 15 minutes until just cooked. Remove from the oven and reduce the heat to 190°C (375°F) Gas 5.

Distribute the stuffing between the mushrooms. Scatter with the pumpkin seeds and a few thyme sprigs. Spoon over a little of the mushroom cooking juices, then return them to the oven for 10 minutes to heat through. To make the sauce, mash the garlic with the salt in a bowl, then gradually work in 3 tablespoons tahini, followed by 1 tablespoon lemon juice. When smooth, gradually work in the yogurt, then taste and add more lemon juice and/or tahini as necessary. Stir in the mint and serve with the mushrooms.

SALADS

spicy vegetable salad

2 large aubergines/eggplant

4 large tomatoes

100 ml/scant ½ cup olive
or argan oil

2–3 garlic cloves, crushed

1 teaspoon harissa paste
(see page 17)

leaves from a small bunch each
of fresh flat leaf parsley and
coriander/cilantro, finely chopped

freshly squeezed juice of 1 lemon

1 teaspoon cumin seeds, roasted
and ground

sea salt and freshly ground
black pepper

crusty bread, to serve

Serves 4

*This classic spicy aubergine/eggplant and tomato salad, is
delicious served on its own with chunks of bread, or as part of
a Moroccan menu. It can be made with olive oil or argan oil,
which is pressed from the nut inside the fruit of the argan tree
indigenous to the Souss region of Morocco.*

Preheat the oven to 200°C (400°F) Gas 6.

Put the aubergines/eggplant on a baking sheet and bake them in the
preheated oven for 30 minutes, until soft when you press them with a
finger. Put the tomatoes in an ovenproof dish, pour over half the olive
oil, and put them in the oven to cook with the aubergines/eggplant.

Remove the aubergines/eggplant and tomatoes from the oven and leave
until cool enough to handle. Using a sharp knife, cut the aubergines/
eggplant in half, scoop out the warm flesh and chop it to a pulp. Skin
the tomatoes, cut them in half, scoop out and discard the seeds and
chop the flesh to a pulp.

Heat the rest of the oil in a heavy-based pan, add the garlic and fry
until it begins to colour, stirring constantly. Add the tomato flesh and
harissa paste and cook over a medium heat for 5–8 minutes, until thick
and pulpy. Add the aubergines/eggplant, parsley and coriander/cilantro.
Stir in the lemon juice and season to taste with salt and pepper. Tip
into a serving bowl and serve warm or at room temperature with a
dusting of roasted cumin and chunks of crusty bread.

roast chicken and minted tabbouleh salad

130 g/⅔ cup bulgur wheat

1 ready-roasted rotisserie chicken

leaves from a large handful each of fresh mint, flat leaf parsley and coriander/cilantro, finely chopped

3 plum tomatoes, halved

2 cucumbers chopped

2 Little Gem lettuces, washed and leaves separated

2 tablespoons freshly squeezed lemon juice

65 ml/⅓ cup olive oil

sea salt and freshly ground black pepper

wholemeal/wholewheat pita breads, to serve

Serves 4

Thankfully, free-range, organic rotisserie chickens are now readily available in larger supermarkets. They are a great way to save time in the kitchen. Shred the flesh and use in soups, pie fillings or to make hearty and delicious salads.

Put the bulgur wheat in a heatproof bowl and pour in 185 ml/ ⅔ cup boiling water. Cover and set aside for 15 minutes. Stir well to fluff the grains up and tip into a larger bowl.

Shred the meat and skin, if liked, of the chicken and put it in the bowl with the bulgur wheat. Add the herbs, tomatoes, cucumbers and lettuce leaves.

Put the lemon juice and olive oil in a small bowl and whisk with a fork to combine. Pour over the salad. Season to taste with salt and pepper and toss to combine all the ingredients. Serve immediately with warmed wholemeal/ wholewheat pita breads on the side.

orange and radish salad with green olives

Oranges are one of the most popular fruits in Moroccan cooking. They are used in refreshing savoury salads, tucked into tagines and served as a sweet salad with orange flower water. As an appetizer, sliced oranges are often combined with black or green olives and a touch of cumin, chilli/chile or paprika in a salad commonly known as meslalla as well as by its literal name, slada bortakal bil zaytoun. This recipe is for a lovely Marrakchi variation on the ever popular theme.

3 sweet oranges, peeled with all the pith removed

12 red radishes, trimmed and thinly sliced or shredded using a mandoline

2 tablespoons green olives, pitted and sliced

2 tablespoons olive oil

freshly squeezed juice of 1 lemon

1 tablespoon orange flower water

2 teaspoons sugar

sea salt and freshly ground black pepper

a few fresh mint leaves, finely shredded, to serve

Serves 4

Cut the oranges into segments on a plate so that you catch the juice. Remove the pith and seeds and cut each segment in half. Put them in a bowl and pour over the juice.

Add the radishes and olives and pour in the olive oil, lemon juice and orange flower water. Add the sugar and season with salt and pepper. Toss the salad lightly, cover and chill in the refrigerator for about 30 minutes.

Toss the salad again before serving and sprinkle with the shredded mint. Serve the salad slightly chilled or at room temperature.

5–6 large tomatoes, skinned, deseeded and cut into thick strips

1 red onion, halved and sliced

rind of 1 preserved lemon, cut into thin strips (see page 13)

2–3 tablespoons olive oil

freshly squeezed juice of ½ lemon

1–2 tablespoons capers, rinsed and drained

leaves from a small bunch each of fresh flat leaf parsley, coriander/cilantro and mint, finely chopped

1 teaspoon paprika

sea salt and freshly ground black pepper

Serves 4–6

preserved lemon and tomato salad with capers

There are a variety of tomato based salads that come under the banner salade marocaine, especially in the tourist areas. This particular recipe is a great favourite on the pied-noir table. Tart, fruity, crunchy and refreshing, it appears in various versions throughout Morocco.

Put the tomatoes, onions and preserved lemon in a bowl. Add the olive oil and lemon juice and toss well. Season with salt and pepper and set aside until ready to serve.

Just before serving, toss in the capers and herbs and scatter the paprika over the top.

roasted peppers with goat cheese, onion and parsley

3 fleshy, red, orange or yellow bell peppers, or combine all 3 colours

2–3 tablespoons argan or olive oil

200 g/2 cups crumbly goat cheese or feta

1 red onion, finely chopped

a small bunch of fresh flat leaf parsley, finely chopped

rind of 1 preserved lemon (see page 13), finely chopped or shredded

Serves 4

This dish can be prepared with colourful bell peppers, or the long, slim, red Mediterranean peppers (ramiro). The sweet and succulent roasted flesh of the peppers is combined with the slightly salty cheese, a crunch of sharp onion and the tangy citrus burst of preserved lemon. It is delicious served as an appetizer or as an accompaniment to grilled meats.

Preheat the oven to 180°C (350°F) Gas 4. Put the peppers in a baking dish, pour over the oil and put them in the oven for about 30 minutes, until the flesh is soft and the skin wrinkly and slightly buckled. Remove from the oven and leave until cool enough to handle. Remove the stalks and peel off the skins. Cut each pepper into quarters lengthways and remove the seeds. Put the peppers on a serving dish.

Crumble the goat cheese over the peppers. Mix the chopped onion with the parsley and scatter the mixture over the peppers. Drizzle the roasting oil over the top and sprinkle with the preserved lemon. Serve while the peppers are still warm or at room temperature.

roasted courgette and apple salad with oranges

The courgette/zucchini is a popular summer squash in Morocco and, as it marries well with fresh herbs and garlic, it appears frequently in salads and dips as well as in vegetable and meat tagines. Served as an appetizer or as a side to a meat and poultry dish, this salad is delightfully refreshing.

2 medium courgettes/zucchini, trimmed, halved and sliced

1 green apple, cored, halved and sliced

3 tablespoons olive oil

freshly squeezed juice of 1 lemon

1 tablespoon dark, clear honey

2 sweet oranges, peeled with pith removed

rind of ½ preserved lemon, finely shredded (see page 13)

leaves from a small bunch of fresh mint, shredded

sea salt

Serves 4–6

Preheat the oven to 200°C (400°F) Gas 6. Put the sliced courgette/zucchini and apple in a baking dish and spoon over the oil. Put them in the oven for about 20 minutes. Take them out and pour over the lemon juice and honey, then put them back for a further 10 minutes, until they have softened and are slightly golden in colour. Leave them to cool in the dish.

Prepare the oranges on a plate to catch the juice. Slice them thinly into neat circles, remove any pips and arrange them on a serving dish. Spoon the roasted courgette/zucchini and apple on top of the oranges. Stir the orange juice that you have caught on the plate into the roasting juices in the baking dish and season with a little salt. Drizzle the juice over the salad and scatter the preserved lemon and mint over the top. Serve chilled or at room temperature.

green olive salad with bitter orange peel

350 g/2 cups fleshy green olives, pitted and cut into slivers

1–2 teaspoons coriander seeds, roasted and crushed

peel of ½ bitter orange or preserved lemon (see page 13), finely chopped or sliced

3 tablespoons olive oil

crusty bread, to serve

Serves 3–4

The most ubiquitous snack or kemia dish in Morocco is a bowl of plump, juicy olives, gleaming in their olive-oil coating and looking resplendent in their varying shades of black, violet, reddish-brown and green. Olives also play a principal role in a number of tagines, dips and salads such as this one, which is generally served on its own with chunks of warm, crusty bread to dip into it. The peel of fresh, or preserved, bitter oranges are used for this dish but if you have difficulty finding bitter oranges, substitute the peel with that of half a preserved lemon.

Tip the olives into a bowl and stir in the coriander seeds and bitter orange peel. Bind with the olive oil, cover and leave to sit for an hour before serving. (You can also make this ahead of time and store it in a sealed container in the refrigerator for 2–3 days). Serve with warm chunks of crusty bread to dip in it.

chickpea salad with onions and paprika

225 g/1 cup dried chickpeas, soaked in plenty of cold water for at least 6 hours

1 red onion, halved and sliced

4 garlic cloves, finely chopped

1 teaspoon ground cumin

1–2 teaspoons paprika

3 tablespoons olive oil

freshly squeezed juice of 1 lemon

a small bunch of fresh flat leaf parsley, coarsely chopped

a small bunch of fresh coriander/cilantro, coarsely chopped

125 g/1¼ cups goat cheese, or feta, crumbled (optional)

sea salt and freshly ground black pepper

crusty bread, to serve

Serves 4

Chickpeas, beans and lentils are consumed daily in rural Morocco, particularly in areas where meat is scarce or expensive. They are cooked in stews, added to couscous, and find their way into salads. This dish is particularly good served warm and is often topped with crumbled goat cheese.

Drain the chickpeas and put them in a deep pan. Cover with water and bring to the boil. Reduce the heat and simmer for about 45 minutes, until the chickpeas are tender but not mushy. Drain the chickpeas and remove any loose skins – you can rub them in a clean tea towel to remove them, or between your fingers.

Tip the warm chickpeas into a bowl. Add the onion, garlic, cumin and paprika and toss in the olive oil and lemon juice while the chickpeas are still warm, making sure they are all well coated. Season with salt and pepper to taste and toss in most of the herbs. Crumble over the goat cheese, if using, and sprinkle with the rest of the herbs. Serve while still warm, with crusty bread.

mixed salad pickles

2 medium carrots, peeled and cut into matchsticks

1–2 white radishes, peeled and cut into matchsticks

1 small cucumber, peeled, deseeded and cut into matchsticks

1 red bell pepper, cut into matchsticks

a few generous pinches of sea salt

2 tablespoons blanched almonds

2 teaspoons pink peppercorns

1–2 teaspoons cumin seeds

a pinch of saffron strands

1–2 cinnamon sticks

freshly squeezed juice of 2–3 lemons

1 tablespoon white vinegar

2 tablespoons sugar

1–2 tablespoons orange flower water

a small bunch of fresh coriander/cilantro, finely chopped

Serves 4–6

One of the most colourful sights in the souks of Fes and Marrakesh are the stacked jars of pickles and preserves. In addition to the ubiquitous preserved lemons, there are a variety of vegetables and fruit such as bitter oranges, aubergines/eggplant, turnips, radishes, peaches, cucumber and beetroot/beets. Often mildly spiced, or spiked with garlic, and sometimes coloured with saffron, pickles and preserves are generally served as an appetizer alongside other salads, or they are enjoyed as a snack with savoury pastries, brochettes or merguez sausages. These salad pickles can be made the day before eating, or they can be stored in a jar in the refrigerator for up to 2 weeks.

Put all the vegetables in a bowl and sprinkle with the salt. Leave to weep for about 30 minutes, then rinse and drain thoroughly.

Tip the vegetables back into the bowl and add the almonds, peppercorns, cumin seeds, saffron and cinnamon sticks. Add the lemon juice, vinegar and sugar and mix well. Cover the bowl and chill in the refrigerator for 6 hours, or overnight.

Before serving, stir in the orange flower water and coriander/cilantro. Serve the pickles at room temperature.

pear and chicory salad with rose petals

Moroccans love to scatter rose petals in salads, over tablecloths and in the small fountains of medinas and riads. Most gardens and courtyards boast several scented rose bushes among the pots of herbs. In this pretty salad, the sweetness of the pear balances the bitterness of the chicory/Belgian endive leaves and both are enhanced by the perfume and floral taste of rose petals.

2–3 ripe but firm pears,
cut into 8 segments and cored

2 white or pink chicory/Belgian
endive, trimmed and leaves
separated

2–3 tablespoons olive or argan oil

freshly squeezed juice of ½ lemon

2 teaspoons dark, clear honey

sea salt and freshly ground
black pepper

a handful of fresh, scented
rose petals

Serves 4–6

Arrange the pear segments and chicory/Belgian endive leaves in a serving bowl. Mix together the oil, lemon juice and honey and season to taste with salt and pepper. Pour the mixture over the salad. Scatter the rose petals over the top and only toss the salad when ready to serve, otherwise the petals become soggy.

watermelon salad with rosewater and lemon balm

When fresh fruit is served at the end of a meal, in most Moroccan households it is usually presented as a salad, or displayed decoratively on a traditional platter. Chopped nuts or fresh herbs, such as lemon balm or mint, are often scattered over the fruit, honey is occasionally drizzled over tart fruit, and the classic rose- and orange flower waters are added for a splash of extra flavour.

1 ripe watermelon, or a large wedge, weighing about 1.5 kg/ 3 lbs. 5 oz.

2 teaspoons sugar

3–4 tablespoons rosewater

a small bunch of fresh lemon balm

Serves 4–6

Remove the skin and seeds from the watermelon. Put the flesh on a plate to catch the juice and cut it into bite-sized cubes. Tip the cubes into a serving bowl and pour over the juice.

Stir the sugar into the rosewater until it has dissolved, and pour the scented mixture over the watermelon. Toss the watermelon lightly, cover the bowl with clingfilm/plastic wrap and chill it in the refrigerator for at least 1 hour.

Toss the watermelon once more before serving, scatter the lemon balm leaves over the top and serve chilled or at room temperature.

SOUPS AND
SMALL BITES

3 tablespoons olive oil plus
1 tablespoon butter, or
3 tablespoons ghee

2 onions, chopped

1 butternut squash, peeled,
and cut into small chunks

4 celery stalks, chopped

2 carrots, peeled and chopped

1–2 teaspoons ground turmeric

2–3 teaspoons ras-el-hanout
(see page 18)

1 tablespoon sugar

2 x 400-g/14-oz. cans chopped
tomatoes, drained of juice

1 tablespoon tomato purée/paste

1.5 litres/6 cups vegetable or
chicken stock

4–5 tablespoons plain yogurt

leaves from a bunch of fresh
coriander/cilantro, roughly
chopped

sea salt and freshly ground
black pepper

bread, to serve

Serves 4–6

rustic tomato and vegetable soup with ras-el-hanout

The thick vegetable soups prepared daily in most homes in Morocco are known as chorba. Often they will suffice as a meal on their own with bread, or they may be served as an appetizer. Chunky and spicy, this is a rustic chorba which, served with a cooling dollop of creamy yogurt, is extremely tasty and satisfying.

Heat the oil and butter in a deep heavy-based saucepan and stir in the onions, squash, celery and carrots. Cook for 4–5 minutes, until the vegetables begin to soften and take on a little colour. Stir in the turmeric, ras-el-hanout and sugar, then add the tomatoes. Stir in the tomato purée/paste and pour in the stock. Bring the liquid to the boil, reduce the heat and simmer for 30–40 minutes, until the vegetables are very tender and the liquid has reduced a little.

Season the soup to taste with salt and pepper and ladle it into warm serving bowls. Swirl a spoonful of yogurt on the top of each serving and sprinkle with the chopped coriander/cilantro. Serve immediately with chunks of warm, crusty bread.

classic lamb, chickpea and lentil soup with cumin

2–3 tablespoons olive or argan oil

2 onions, chopped

2 celery stalks, diced

2 small carrots, peeled and diced

2–3 garlic cloves, left whole and smashed

1 tablespoon cumin seeds

450 g/1 lb. lean, boned lamb, cut into bite-sized cubes

2–3 teaspoons ground turmeric

2 teaspoons paprika

2 teaspoons ground cinnamon

2 teaspoons sugar

2 bay leaves

2 tablespoons tomato purée/paste

1 litre/4 cups lamb or chicken stock

1 x 400-g/14-oz. can chickpeas,

1 x 400-g/14-oz. can chopped tomatoes, drained of juice

100 g/½ cup brown or green lentils,

a small bunch of fresh flat leaf parsley, coarsely chopped

a small bunch of fresh coriander/cilantro, coarsely chopped

sea salt and freshly ground black pepper

crusty bread, to serve

Serves 4–6

Variations of this soup can be found throughout the Islamic world. In Morocco alone there are at least a dozen versions, differentiated by their regional recipes and by the vegetables used in the soup. It is one of the classic dishes prepared at religious feasts and it is traditionally served to break the fast during Ramadan, the month of fasting. Thick and hearty, with a consistency that comes somewhere between a soup and a stew, it can be served as a meal on its own with thick, crusty bread, flat bread or with rustic semolina rolls.

Heat the oil in a deep, heavy-based saucepan. Stir in the onions, celery and carrots and cook until the onions begin to colour. Add the smashed garlic and cumin seeds and toss in the lamb. Cook until lightly browned. Add the spices, sugar and bay leaves and stir in the tomato purée/paste. Pour in the stock and bring the liquid to the boil. Reduce the heat, cover with a lid, and simmer for 1 hour, until the meat is tender.

Add the chopped tomatoes, chickpeas and lentils to the pan and cook gently for a further 30 minutes, until the lentils are soft and the soup is almost as thick as a stew. Top up with a little water, if necessary, as the lentils will absorb most of it. Season the soup with salt and pepper and add most of the parsley and coriander/cilantro.

Serve the soupy stew hot, sprinkled with the remaining parsley and coriander/cilantro with plenty of bread for dipping.

fish soup with lemon and harissa

2–3 tablespoons olive oil

1 onion, finely chopped

2 celery stalks, diced

2–3 garlic cloves, finely chopped

1–2 teaspoons harissa paste (see page 17)

a small bunch of fresh flat leaf parsley, finely chopped

1 litre/4 cups fish stock or water

freshly squeezed juice of 2 lemons

1 glass fino sherry or white wine

1 x 400-g/14-oz. can of chopped tomatoes, drained of juice

1 kg/2 lb. 4 oz. firm-fleshed fish, such as cod, haddock, ling, grouper, sea bass or snapper, cut into large chunks

500 g/1 lb. 2 oz. shellfish, such as prawns/shrimp, clams and mussels, cleaned and in their shells

leaves from a small bunch of fresh coriander/cilantro, coarsely chopped

sea salt and freshly ground black pepper

bread or Plain, Buttery Couscous (see page 103), to serve

Serves 4–6

Although Morocco boasts an extensive coastline, there are few fish soups on the national menu, as the bulk of the daily catch is grilled in the streets, baked with dates or olives or simmered with herbs and spices in tagines. However, in some of the northern coastal areas, such as Casablanca, Tangier and Tetouan, there are a few gems that echo the well-flavoured soupy stews of Mediterranean Spain and France. Soups of this nature are often best served on their own with plenty of crusty bread, or spooned over Plain, Buttery Couscous.

Heat the oil in a deep, heavy based saucepan, stir in the onion, celery and garlic and fry gently until it begins to colour. Add the harissa paste and parsley and pour in the stock. Bring the liquid to the boil, reduce the heat and simmer for 10 minutes to allow the flavours to mingle.

Add the lemon juice and fino sherry, and stir in the tomatoes. Season to taste with salt and pepper. Gently stir in the fish chunks and shellfish and bring the liquid to the boil again. Reduce the heat and simmer for 3–4 minutes, until the fish is cooked through. Sprinkle the chopped coriander/cilantro over the top and serve immediately with lots of bread or Plain, Buttery Couscous.

harrira

2 tablespoons extra virgin olive oil

a 450-g/1-lb. lamb shank

2 onions, sliced

3 celery stalks, chopped

3 garlic cloves, chopped

1 teaspoon ground cinnamon

½ teaspoon saffron strands

½ teaspoon ground ginger

several gratings of nutmeg

1 tablespoon tomato purée/paste

4 tomatoes, chopped

700 ml/scant 3 cups lamb stock or water

200 g/scant 3 cups canned chickpeas,

100 g/½ cup green lentils

freshly squeezed juice of 1 lemon

2 tablespoons freshly chopped coriander/cilantro

sea salt and freshly ground black pepper

Serves 4–6

This is a soup sold all over Morocco. At Ramadan, when most of the country is fasting, there is an eerie silence in the usually bustling souks as stall vendors tuck into their harrira, their first meal of the day at sundown. It can be as rustic as you like but my version is defined by the subtle flavour of saffron and accompanying spices. Generally it has a little meat, tomatoes and lots of spices. Some people stir in some egg at the end, or a fermented batter of flour and water, and I have even seen it with vermicelli and rice, but the way I like to make it, I find it thick enough without any of these.

Heat the olive oil in a heavy-based casserole dish, then add the lamb and brown evenly. Add the onions, celery, garlic, cinnamon, saffron, ginger and nutmeg and season with salt and pepper. Turn the heat down a little, cover and cook for 10 minutes until soft, stirring occasionally.

Stir in the tomato purée/paste and the tomatoes and cook for a further 2–3 minutes. Add the stock, cover and cook for 1 hour until the lamb is becoming tender.

Add the chickpeas and lentils and cook for a further 40 minutes until they are tender and the lamb can easily be pulled off the bone. Shred the meat from the shank, remove the bone and discard. Add lemon juice to taste and check the seasoning (it needs quite a generous amount of salt). Stir in the coriander/cilantro and serve immediately.

450 g/1 lb. cooked white fish
fillets, such as sea bass or
haddock, skinned
and flaked

1–2 teaspoons harissa paste
(see page 17)

rind of ½ a preserved lemon,
finely chopped (see page 13)

a small bunch of fresh coriander/
cilantro, chopped

a pinch of saffron strands,
soaked in 1 teaspoon water
to draw out the colour

2 teaspoons dark, clear honey

1 egg

fresh breadcrumbs from 2 slices
bread, crusts removed

2 tablespoons plain/all-purpose
flour

sunflower oil, for frying

sea salt and freshly ground
black pepper

1 lemon, cut into wedges, to serve

Serves 4

mini fish kefta
with saffron

*One of the joys of the street food in the coastal towns, such
as Essaouira, is the aroma of grilled or fried fish cooking
with spices as the fish kefta or brochettes are prepared for
passers-by. Mini fish kefta are often served as an appetizer
accompanied by a salad, a dip and a bowl of olives.*

Put the fish in a bowl and add the harissa paste, preserved lemon,
coriander/cilantro, saffron and honey. Beat in the egg, season with
salt and pepper, and add enough breadcrumbs to bind the mixture.
Knead the mixture with your hand and take small apricot-sized
lumps into your palms to mould them into small balls. Roll the
balls lightly in the flour.

Heat the oil in a heavy-based pan and fry the balls in batches for
3–4 minutes, until golden brown all over. Drain them on paper
towels and serve hot with wedges of lemon for squeezing.

savoury pastries filled with spicy meat

1–2 tablespoons olive oil

1 onion, finely chopped

2 tablespoons blanched almonds, chopped

1 teaspoon ras-el-hanout (see page 18)

225 g/8 oz. finely minced/ ground beef

8 sheets filo/phyllo pastry

sunflower oil, for deep-frying

salt and freshly ground black pepper

Serves 4–6

Briouats are little savoury pastries that can be filled with a variety of ingredients, such as saffron-flavoured chicken, spinach or spicy ground lamb or beef. Popular as street food, or as hot starters, briouats are as familiar a sight as skewers or brochettes.

Heat the oil in a heavy-based pan and stir in the onion and the chopped almonds. Just as they begin to colour, stir in the ras-el-hanout. Add the beef and cook until well browned and cooked through. Season to taste with salt and pepper and let cool.

Lay the sheets of filo/phyllo on a flat surface, cut them into strips about 8–10 cm/4 inches wide and cover them with a damp cloth. Take a strip and spoon a little of the filling mixture on the short end nearest to you. Fold the corners over the mixture to seal it, then roll it away from you into a tight cigar shape. As you reach the end of the strip, brush it with a little water and continue to roll. Repeat with the remaining strips and filling. Keep the pastries covered with a damp cloth to prevent them from drying out before you are ready to cook them.

Heat sufficient sunflower oil for deep-frying in a saucepan and fry the cigars over a medium heat, until golden brown. Drain on paper towels and serve warm.

pastry triangles filled with tuna and egg

Popular street food in the coastal areas, these tuna and egg-filled pastries are originally from neighbouring Tunisia, but have been adopted by the Moroccans. As the egg is designed to be runny inside the pastry, there is an art to eating them by holding the corners of the pastry as you bite into the middle.

1 tablespoon olive oil

1 onion, finely chopped

6–8 anchovy fillets

1 x 200-g/7-oz. can of tuna, drained

1 tablespoon capers, rinsed and drained

a small bunch fresh flat leaf parsley, finely chopped

2 sheets filo/phyllo pastry, cut into
4 x 20-cm/8-inch squares

4 eggs

sunflower oil, for shallow frying

Serves 4

Heat the oil in a frying pan and stir in the onions for 2 minutes to soften them. Add the anchovies and fry gently until they melt into the oil. Turn off the heat and leave the mixture to cool. Tip the cooked onion mixture into a bowl and add the tuna. Break up the tuna with a fork and add the capers and parsley. Mix well to combine.

Place the filo/phyllo squares on a work surface and spoon one quarter of the mixture onto one half of a square in the shape of a triangle. Make a well in the tuna mixture and crack an egg into it. Fold the empty side of the filo/phyllo over the filling, taking care not to move or break the yolk of the egg, and then seal the edges with a little water. Repeat with the 3 other pastry squares.

Heat sufficient oil for shallow frying in a heavy-based frying pan and slip one of the pastries into the oil. Fry for less than 1 minute on each side. When crisp and golden brown, carefully lift the pastry out of the pan using a slotted spoon and drain it on paper towels. Repeat with the other pastries and serve warm while the yolk is still runny.

baked pastries with seafood

15 g/½ oz. fresh yeast

400 ml/1⅓ cups lukewarm water

350 g plain/all-purpose flour

1 teaspoon salt

175 ml/⅓ cup sunflower oil, plus extra for working the dough

1 egg yolk mixed with 1tablespoon water, for brushing

FOR THE FILLING:

freshly squeezed juice of 3 lemons

175 g/6 oz. small fresh prawns/shrimp, shelled and deveined

175 g/6 oz. small squid, with ink sack, back bone and head removed, and thinly sliced

2–3 tablespoons olive oil plus 1 tablespoon butter

2 onions, finely chopped

2 garlic cloves, crushed

1 fresh red or green chilli/chile, finely chopped

1 teaspoon ground cumin

1 teaspoon ground coriander

1 teaspoon paprika

a bunch of fresh coriander/cilantro, finely chopped

a bunch of fresh flat leaf parsley, finely chopped

sea salt and freshly ground black pepper

Serves 4–6

This is a delicious seafood pastry that you can watch being assembled in front of you at some of the seafront restaurants in the pretty blue and white coastal town, Essaouira, where they are cooked on makeshift griddles. At home, you can use a griddle/stove-top grill pan or bake them in the oven.

In a small bowl, cream the yeast with roughly 100 ml/scant ½ cup of the warm water and leave it in a warm place until frothy. Sift the flour and the salt into a wide-rimmed bowl and make a well in the centre. Pour the oil and the yeast mixture into the well. Gradually, add the remaining water as you draw the flour in from the sides of the bowl and knead the mixture with your hands to form a smooth, soft dough. Divide the dough into 12 equal balls, place them on a lightly oiled surface and cover with a damp tea towel. Leave to prove for about 1 hour, until they have doubled in size.

Meanwhile, prepare the filling. Bring a pan of water and half the lemon juice to the boil. Drop in the prawns/shrimp and squid, cook for 2–3 minutes, then drain and refresh under cold running water. Set aside. Heat the olive oil and butter in a heavy-based pan and stir in the onions, garlic and chilli/chile. Cook for for 2–3 minutes, until they begin to colour. Stir in the spices and toss in the cooked prawns/shrimp and squid. Add the herbs and the rest of the lemon juice and season to taste with salt and pepper. Turn off the heat and leave the mixture to cool.

Preheat the oven to 180°C (350°F) Gas 4. Take a ball of dough, put it on a lightly oiled surface, then spread and stretch it with your fingers to form a thin circle about 12–15 cm/5–6 inches diameter. Repeat with the remaining balls of dough. Put a large spoonful of the seafood mixture just off centre in each circle. Fold the narrower edge over the mixture, tuck in the ends, then fold the wider edge over to seal in the mixture and form a square package. Place the pastries sealed-side down on an oiled baking sheet and brush them with a little of the egg yolk mixture. Bake the pastries for about 30 minutes, until golden, and serve immediately.

SWEET THINGS
AND DRINKS

prunes stuffed with walnuts in spiced orange syrup

450 g/4 cups pitted, ready-to-eat prunes

225 g/2 cups shelled walnuts

freshly squeezed juice of 2 oranges

1–2 tablespoons orange flower water

4 tablespoons granulated sugar

1–2 teaspoons ground cinnamon

Serves 4–6

In Morocco, prunes and dates are often stuffed with walnuts, almonds or marzipan, and are generally served as a dessert or sweet snack. Poached in an orange syrup with a dusting of cinnamon, they are delicious served as the perfect finish to a Moroccan menu.

Using a sharp knife, slit the prunes open to create a pouch and stuff a walnut into each one. Put the stuffed prunes in the base of a tagine or a heavy-based casserole dish. Pour over the orange juice and orange flower water and sprinkle with the sugar. Cover with a lid and simmer over low heat for about 20 minutes, basting the juice over the prunes from time to time. Sprinkle the cinnamon over the top and serve hot, or at room temperature.

gazelle's horns

250 g/2 cups plain/all-purpose flour, plus extra for dusting

a pinch of salt

2 tablespoons sunflower oil, plus extra for brushing

100 ml/scant 1 cup orange flower water, plus extra for sprinkling

100 ml/scant 1 cup water

icing/confectioners' sugar, for dusting

FOR THE ALMOND FILLING:

300 g/2 cups ground almonds

300 g/1½ cups caster sugar

2 eggs, lightly beaten

3–4 tablespoons orange flower water

1 teaspoon ground cinnamon

Almond Milk (see page 233), to serve

Makes 25–30 pastries

Said to resemble the horns of the antelope that roam the Atlas mountains, these sickle-moon shaped pastries are a delightful treat. Traditionally, they are served as a gift to guests with a glass of mint tea or a cold drink, such as Almond Milk.

Preheat the oven to 180°C (350°F) Gas 4. First, prepare the filling. Put all the filling ingredients in a large bowl and, using your hand, work them into a stiff paste. Take a small portion of the mixture into your hands and roll it into a log, approximately 8 cm/3½ inches long. Continue with the rest of the mixture until you have 25–30 logs. Brush them lightly with sunflower oil as you make them so that they remain moist. Set aside.

To prepare the pastry, sift the flour and salt into a bowl. Make a well in the centre and pour in the oil, orange flower water and water. Using your fingers, draw in the flour from the outside of the bowl to form a dough. Knead the dough for about 10 minutes, until it is soft and springy. Transfer the dough to a lightly floured surface and roll it out to form a large rectangle, about 2 mm/½ inch thick. Place 3 almond logs along the long side, 5 cm/ 2 inches from the edge and leaving a 5 cm/2 inch gap between them. Brush the edges of the pastry and around the almond logs with water. Fold the edge over the almond logs and press the dough around the filling to keep it in place. Using a fluted pastry wheel, carefully cut a half moon, starting from the folded edge, around the filling, and back down to the folded edge again, so that you end up with three half circles. Repeat with the rest of the pastry, until you have roughly 25 half-circle shaped pastries. Place a finger in the middle of the bottom edge of each pastry and, carefully, press the filling upwards to shape the pastry into a crescent moon, or a gazelle's horn.

Place the gazelle's horns onto a lightly oiled baking sheet and prick each one with a fork. Bake them in the preheated oven for 15–20 minutes until lightly browned. Transfer them to a wire rack, brush with a little orange flower water and dust with icing/confectioners' sugar while still hot. Serve warm or at room temperature.

classic 'snake' pastry with almond filling

125 g/4½ oz. filo/phyllo pastry
(about 5–6 sheets)

60 g/4 tablespoons butter, melted

1 egg yolk, mixed with
1 tablespoon water

2–3 tablespoons icing/
confectioners' sugar,
plus extra for sprinkling

FOR THE ALMOND FILLING:

350 g/2¼ cups ground almonds

225 g/1 cup 2 tablespoons
caster/granulated sugar

50 g/½ cup icing/confectioners'
sugar

1 tablespoon ground cinnamon,
plus extra for decorating

2–3 tablespoons orange
flower water

2 teaspoons ground cinnamon

Serves 8–10

Coiled like a snake, this is the most stunning of Morocco's sweet pastries. Literally translated from Arabic as 'snake', m'hanncha is crisp and buttery and filled with an exquisite scented almond paste. Traditionally m'hanncha is served on festive occasions, accompanied by a glass of Mint Tea or Almond Milk.

Preheat the oven to 180°C (350°F) Gas 4. To make the filling, put all the ingredients for the filling in a large bowl and work them with your hands to form a stiff paste. Take a lump of the paste out of the bowl and roll it on a flat surface to form a finger that is roughly 1.5 cm/¾ inch thick and about 8 cm/3½ inches long. Repeat with the remaining filling. Cover and chill in the refrigerator for 30 minutes.

Line a round baking pan or a wide baking sheet with a piece of kitchen foil then place it and the filo/phyllo sheets beside your work surface. Make sure you keep the filo/phyllo in a stack covered with a damp cloth while working with them. Take the first sheet of filo/phyllo and place it on the surface, with the longer side nearest to you. Lightly brush the top of it with a little melted butter and place several of the almond fingers, end to end, along the edge nearest to you. Roll the nearest edge up over the filling, tuck in the ends, and roll it into a long, thin tube. Gently push both ends of the tube towards the centre so that it creases, then place it on top of the foil in the middle of the baking pan. Carefully curve it around into a coil.

Repeat the process with the other sheets of filo/phyllo, until all the almond mixture fingers are used up and the pastry resembles a coiled snake. Brush the top of the pastry with the egg yolk mixture and bake it in the oven for 30–35 minutes, until crisp and lightly browned. Take the pastry out of the oven and sprinkle it liberally with icing/confectioners' sugar. Decorate the top by rubbing the ground cinnamon between your thumb and index finger to create thin lines from the centre to the outer rim of the pastry snake, like the spokes of a wheel. Serve while still warm, or at room temperature.

semolina pancakes with honey

15 g/½ oz. fresh yeast

125 ml/½ cup lukewarm water

225 g/2¼ cups fine semolina

250 g/2 cups plain/all-purpose flour

½ teaspoon sea salt

2 eggs

125 ml/½ cup lukewarm milk

sunflower oil, for shallow frying

50 g/3½ tablespoons unsalted butter

200 ml/⅔ cup scented dark, clear honey

FOR THE COMPOTE:

250 g/1⅔ cups dried, ready-to-eat apricots

250 g/2 cups pitted, ready-to-eat prunes

125 g/scant 1 cup sultanas/golden raisins

125 g/scant 1 cup blanched almonds

175 g/¾ cup plus 2 tablespoons caster/granulated sugar

2–3 tablespoons orange flower water

1–2 cinnamon sticks

Serves 4–6

These light, airy pancakes are a great favourite in Morocco for breakfast or a sweet snack. Bubbly on one side, smooth on the other, they melt deliciously in the mouth with a drizzle of honey, lashings of butter or a sprinkling of sugar and cinnamon.

First, prepare the fruit compote. Put the dried fruit and almonds in a bowl and pour in just enough water to cover the fruit and nuts. Gently stir in the sugar and orange flower water and add the cinnamon stick. Cover the bowl and chill it in the refrigerator for 48 hours, during which time the water and sugar will form a golden syrup.

Put the yeast in a bowl with the lukewarm water and leave it in a warm place until it dissolves and becomes frothy.

Sift the semolina, flour and salt into a large bowl. Make a well in the centre. Beat the eggs into the milk and pour the mixture into the well. Tip in the yeast mixture and, using a wooden spoon, draw in the flour from the sides of the bowl. Beat the mixture for about 5 minutes, until light and smooth. Cover the bowl with a clean kitchen towel and leave to prove in a warm place for at least 2 hours.

To make the pancakes, heat a non-stick frying pan and wipe it with a little oil. Pour a small ladleful of batter into the middle of the pan and spread it a little to form a thick round about 12–14 cm/5–6 inches in diameter. Cook the pancake until the surface looks dry and is perforated with bubbles. Lift it out of the pan and transfer to a heated plate and cover to keep warm while you cook the remaining pancakes in the same way.

Melt the butter and heat the honey in separate pans. Drizzle the butter over the pancakes and serve immediately with the warm honey and fruit compote for drizzling.

rose-flavoured milk pudding

60 g/⅓ cup plus 1 tablespoon rice flour

1 litre/4 cups whole or semi-skimmed milk

125 g/½ cup plus 2 tablespoons caster/granulated sugar

2–3 tablespoons rosewater

1–2 tablespoons icing/confectioners' sugar

Serves 4–6

Silky and light, this traditional pudding is a classic throughout North Africa and the Middle East, as the recipe travelled with the invading Arabs across the region. Often served at religious feasts, it can be flavoured with rosewater or orange flower water and a generous dusting of icing/confectioners' sugar.

In a small bowl, mix the rice flour with a little of the milk to form a loose paste. Pour the rest of the milk into a heavy-based saucepan and stir in the sugar. Bring the milk to boiling point, stirring all the time, until the sugar has dissolved. Reduce the heat and stir a spoonful or two of the hot milk into the rice flour paste, then tip the mixture into the pan, stirring all the time to prevent the flour from forming lumps. Bring the milk back to boiling point and stir in the rosewater. Reduce the heat to low and simmer gently for 20–25 minutes, stirring from time to time, until the mixture becomes quite thick and coats the back of the spoon.

Pour the mixture into a large serving bowl, or individual ones, and leave to cool, allowing a skin to form on top. Chill in the refrigerator and dust with icing/confectioners' sugar before serving.

candied aubergines

The tradition of candied fruit and vegetables is popular throughout North Africa and the Middle East, where the variety ranges from watermelon, plum tomatoes, carrots, quinces, grapefruit peel, clementines, lemons, sweet potatoes, courgettes/zucchini to baby aubergines/eggplant. These are delicious served as a treat at the end of a special meal with a glass of Mint Tea.

8–12 firm baby aubergines/
eggplant, stalk intact

225 ml/scant 1 cup water

450 g/2¼ cups caster/
superfine sugar

freshly squeezed juice of 1 lemon

5 cm/2 inches fresh ginger,
peeled and thinly sliced

2 cinnamon sticks

6 cloves

2 pieces mace

1 piece mastic* the size
of a small coin

Serves 4

Prick the aubergines/eggplant all over with a fork and put them in a steamer. Steam for 15 minutes, drain off any water and leave them to cool.

Meanwhile, make the syrup. Pour the water into a heavy-based saucepan. Reserve 1 teaspoon of the sugar, then add the remainder to the pan with the lemon juice. Bring the water to the boil, stirring all the time, until the sugar has dissolved. Add the ginger and spices, reduce the heat and simmer gently for 10 minutes, until the syrup is thick and coats the back of the spoon. Crush the mastic with the reserved teaspoon of sugar and stir it into the syrup.

Gently squeeze the aubergines/eggplant to remove any excess water and place them in the syrup. Cook the aubergines/eggplant in the syrup, partially covered, over very low heat for about 1 hour, making sure they are submerged in the syrup and that the sugar doesn't burn and catch on the bottom of the pan.

Remove the pan from the heat and leave the aubergines/eggplant to cool in the syrup. Arrange the aubergines/eggplant on a serving dish with the stalks pointing upwards. Strain the syrup and drizzle it over them before serving. Alternatively, you can store them in the strained syrup in a sealed, sterilized jar for several months.

*Mastic is a resin obtained from the mastic tree that grows throughout the Mediterranean. It's mainly used as a flavouring and for its 'gum' properties. It can be bought from specialist Greek stores.

fresh figs with walnuts and honey

4–5 tablespoons walnuts

8 fresh, ripe figs

4–5 tablespoons scented, dark, clear honey

Serves 4

Moroccans believe that figs aid digestion so, when in season, they are often served fresh at the end of a meal. There are many delicious varieties of scented honey in Morocco, such as thyme and lavender and the honey of 1,000 flowers (mille-fleurs). There is also a special honey called jbal that is particularly sweet and delicate as it is made by bees that only feast on figs.

Preheat the oven to 160°C (325°F) Gas 3.

Put the walnuts on a baking sheet and roast in the oven, until they emit a nutty aroma and deepen in colour. Using a mortar and pestle, or an electric blender, grind the walnuts coarsely.

Using a sharp knife, slit open each fig by cutting it from the top into quarters, but make sure you don't cut through the base, so that the fruit opens like a flower. Arrange the figs on a serving dish. Drizzle the honey over each one and scatter the toasted walnuts over the fruit and around the dish. Serve immediately.

yogurt and pistachio cake

Pistachio nuts are used in traditional desserts throughout North Africa and the Middle East. In this recipe, the crunchy texture of the nuts perfectly complements the velvety sweetness of the cake. Similar to a cheesecake, this light, fluffy dessert is best served cold or chilled.

3 eggs, separated

85 g/scant ½ cup caster/granulated sugar

60 ml/¼ cup sour cream

1½ tablespoons plain/all-purpose flour

250 g/1 cup plain yogurt

grated zest and freshly squeezed juice of 1 unwaxed lemon

1–2 drops vanilla extract, to taste

25 g/¼ cup pistachio nuts, chopped

a medium ovenproof baking dish

Serves 8

Put the egg yolks and 60 g/⅓ cup of the sugar in a large bowl and whisk for a couple of minutes until thick and pale. In a separate bowl, stir together the sour cream and flour until well mixed, then fold in the yogurt, lemon zest and juice, and vanilla extract to taste. Stir this mixture into the whisked egg yolks.

In a separate, large, grease-free bowl, whisk the egg whites until they form stiff peaks, then sprinkle in the remaining sugar and whisk until very stiff and glossy. Add the yogurt and egg yolk mixture and gently fold together. Pour or spoon the mixture into a baking dish.

Place the dish in a roasting pan. Pour in sufficient cold water to reach about halfway up the sides of the dish, then bake for 20 minutes. Carefully slide the dish out of the oven, sprinkle the cake with the nuts and return it to the oven to bake for a further 15–20 minutes, until a golden colour and firm to the touch.

Remove the cake from the oven and let cool. Chill in the refrigerator before serving.

honeyed couscous with fresh figs and rosewater cream

In Morocco, sweet couscous is one of the most popular snacks and is also enjoyed as a nourishing breakfast, served with a variety of dried fruits and nuts and plenty of honey and cream for drizzling. This variation of the traditional recipe and makes a deliciously different and indulgent dessert.

140 g/⅔ cup couscous

1 tablespoon unsalted butter

2 tablespoons dark, clear honey

½ teaspoon ground cinnamon

4–6 fresh figs, halved

1 teaspoon golden caster/granulated sugar

125 ml/½ cup double/heavy cream

2 tablespoons light soft brown sugar

½ teaspoon rosewater

Serves 4

Put the couscous in a heatproof bowl and set aside.

Put the butter, honey, cinnamon and 125 ml/½ cup cold water in a small saucepan and set over high heat. As soon as the mixture boils, pour it over the couscous, quickly stir just to combine and cover tightly with clingfilm/plastic wrap. Let sit for 10 minutes, then fluff up with a fork, making certain to pick up the grains at the bottom of the bowl. Re-cover and let sit for 5–10 minutes more. When cool enough to handle, use your fingertips to fluff and aerate the grains.

Preheat the grill/broiler to high. Sprinkle the caster/granulated sugar over the cut sides of the figs and cook under the grill/broiler, until the sugar is golden and the figs have softened just slightly.

Put the cream, brown sugar and rosewater in a bowl and stir to combine. Spoon the couscous into serving bowls, arrange a few figs on top and add a spoonful of the rosewater cream. Serve immediately.

date, pistachio and coconut truffles

250 g/2½ cups shelled pistachios

250 g/1½ cups pitted ready-to-eat dates, roughly chopped

1–2 tablespoons orange flower water

1–2 teaspoons ground cinnamon

1 tablespoon dark, clear honey

200 g/2½ cups desiccated coconut

Mint Tea (see page 230), to serve

Makes 15–20 small truffles

The nomadic Berbers rely heavily on dates as a main source of food and many traditional dishes include them – lamb tagines, couscous and a variety of sweets, such as these truffles. Generally, in the home, these succulent truffles are one of the delicacies traditionally offered to guests with a glass of Mint Tea.

Toast the pistachios in a heavy-based frying pan, or roast them in a medium oven on a baking sheet, until they emit a lovely nutty aroma. Using a mortar and pestle, or an electric blender, grind the pistachios. Add the dates and pound them with the ground pistachios to form a thick paste.

Spoon the date and pistachio paste into a bowl and, using your hands, mix in the orange flower water, cinnamon and honey. Shape the mixture into 15–20 small, bite-sized balls. Sprinkle the coconut onto a plate or flat surface and then roll the sticky balls in it, until evenly coated.

Arrange the truffles in a serving dish and serve with traditional Mint Tea. They can be stored in an airtight container in the refrigerator for 1 week. Serve them at room temperature.

fluffy pistachio nougat

300 g/3 cups shelled pistachios

300 ml/1¼ cups water

900 g/4½ cups caster sugar

1 piece mastic the size of a small coin (see page 218)

freshly squeezed juice of 2 lemons

4 egg whites

2 tablespoons shelled, unsalted pistachios, finely ground, to decorate (optional)

Serves 8–10

A variety of soft and hard nougats made with sesame seeds, sunflower seeds, peanuts, almonds, pistachios and pumpkin seeds are sold in the streets and souks. This soft nougat, which employs mastic for its chewy twang and mild, resinous flavour, is traditionally served in Jewish households to celebrate the end of Passover, but throughout Morocco it is hugely popular with children.

Toast the pistachios in a heavy-based frying pan, or roast them in a medium oven on a baking sheet, until they emit a lovely nutty aroma. Using a mortar and pestle, or an electric blender, crush the roasted pistachios coarsely.

Pour the water into a heavy-based saucepan. Reserve 1 teaspoon of the sugar and add the remainder to the pan. Bring the mixture to the boil, stirring all the time, until the sugar has dissolved. Reduce the heat and simmer gently for about 10 minutes, until the syrup coats the back of the wooden spoon – the syrup should be thick and transparent.

Using a small mortar and pestle, grind the mastic with the reserved teaspoon of sugar and add it, with the lemon juice, to the syrup. Take the pan off the heat and cool the syrup down by beating it continuously, until warm to the touch.

Whisk the egg whites in a bowl until thick and frothy and then fold them, one spoonful at a time, into the warm syrup. Place the pan over low heat and stir for 5 minutes. Gradually add the crushed pistachios, making sure they are well dispersed throughout the mixture. Tip the mixture into a large serving bowl, or individual serving bowls, and leave to cool. Decorate with a sprinkling of finely ground pistachios and serve while it is still just warm, or at room temperature.

mint tea

1–1½ tablespoons dried Chinese green tea leaves

a handful of fresh mint leaves on their stalks

about 12 sugar lumps

Serves 4–6

Mint tea, Morocco's national drink, is offered throughout the day in people's homes, in cafés and restaurants, in the markets, at the end of a meal and just about anywhere you go. It is prepared by brewing Chinese green tea with a handful of scented mint leaves and large amounts of sugar to satisfy the sweet-toothed Moroccans and it is served with a flourish, poured from a height into decorative glasses.

Pour some boiling water into a teapot to warm it. Swirl the water around and pour it out. Put the tea, mint and sugar in the pot and pour over more boiling water. Stir the tea until the mint rises to the surface and the sugar has dissolved. Leave the tea to infuse for 5 minutes.

Place the tea glasses side by side, hold the teapot just above the first glass and, as you pour, raise the teapot higher to create a little froth on the surface. Continue with the other glasses and serve hot to accompany any of the delectable Moroccan pastries or sweets.

almond milk

250 g/1⅔ cups blanched almonds

125 g/½ cup plus 2 tablespoons caster sugar

600 ml/scant 2½ cups water

1–2 tablespoons orange flower water

rose petals, orange zest or ground cinnamon, to serve

Serves 4

Almond milk is a classic North African and Middle Eastern drink. Served chilled on a hot day, it is both nourishing and refreshing. Traditionally, the 'milk' is extracted from the almonds, but modern recipes often add cow's milk. In Morocco, orange flower water or fresh orange rind are added to the drink to give it a floral or zesty lift and, on special occasions, rose petals are floated on the surface of each glass.

Using a mortar and pestle, or an electric blender, pound the almonds with half the sugar to a smooth paste – add a splash of water if the paste gets too stiff.

Put the water and the remaining sugar in a heavy-based saucepan and bring it to the boil, stirring until the sugar has dissolved. Stir in the almond paste and simmer for 5 minutes.

Turn off the heat and stir in the orange flower water. Leave the mixture to cool in the pan to enable the flavours to mingle. Once cool, strain the mixture through a muslin cloth, or a fine, plastic sieve/strainer (don't use a metal one as it will taint the flavour and colour of the almonds). Use your hand to squeeze all the milk out of the almonds.

Pour the cloudy liquid into a jug/pitcher and chill in the refrigerator. When ready to serve, give it a stir and pour the milk into glasses over ice cubes, or place the glasses in the freezer so they are frosty when served. Decorate with rose petals, a fine curl of orange zest, or a pinch of ground cinnamon.

orange blossom cocktail

400 ml/1½ cups orange-infused vodka

a splash of freshly squeezed lemon juice

a splash of freshly squeezed orange juice

1—2 drops orange flower water

40 ml/3 tablespoons apricot nectar/juice

50 ml/4 tablespoons unfiltered apple juice

slice of orange, to garnish

Serves 5

Oranges and other citrus fruits are often used in Moroccan and North African cuisine, as oranges and lemons are readily available throughout the region. This refreshingly fruity cocktail is perfect for entertaining.

Put all the ingredients in a shaker filled with ice and shake. Pour into a Moroccan tea glass or tumbler to serve.

index

recipe credits

All recipes by Ghillie Basan except those on pages 112, 168, 225, by Ross Dobson, page 222 by Susannah Blake, page 75 by Laura Washburn, page160 by Jennifer Joyce, p163 by Brian Glover, page 196 by Tonia George.

photography credits

key: r=right, l=left, c=centre, a=above, b=below

Steve Baxter
Page 104 background

Henry Bourne
Page 63 inset

Martin Brigdale
Pages 2, 4, 10r, 13 inset, 18 inset, 22, 25, 29–30, 33–34, 39 inset, 40, 43–44, 47–48, 51, 54, 57–58, 62, 65–66, 69–70, 73–75, 77, 81, 83–84, 85 inset, 87–88, 91–92, 93 inset, 95–96, 99, 109, 125 inset, 141 inset, 172 inset, 188, 222 inset, 223, 225 inset

Peter Cassidy
Pages 1, 3, 5–6, 7 inset, 8 inset, 9, 10ab, 12, 15–16, 19–20, 21 inset, 26, 27 inset, 31–32, 37–38, 50, 53 inset, 61, 68, 78, 82, 100–102, 103 inset, 104 inset, 105–106, 107 inset, 110, 114–116, 119, 127–128, 130 inset, 131–132, 134–136, 138 inset, 139–140, 143–146, 149–150, 152–154, 157–158, 161–162, 164–166, 168, 170, 171 inset, 173–175, 176 inset, 177–178, 181–182, 185–186, 189–190, 193–195, 198,

201–202, 203 inset, 205–208, 209 inset, 211–212, 215–216, 218 inset, 219–221, 224, 227–228, 230 inset, 231–232

Nicki Dowie
Page 35

Richard Jung
Pages 17, 42, 49, 60 inset, 94, 113, 120–124, 142 inset, 147 background

Lisa Linder
Page 59

William Lingwood
Pages 138 background, 147 inset, 183, 234 inset

Diana Miller
Pages 36 inset, 72, 89, 133 inset, 160 inset, 187 inset

Gloria Nicol
Page 184 inset

William Reavell
Pages 18 background, 23, 41, 55, 60 background, 76, 103 background, 118 inset, 125 background, 130 background, 142 background, 148, 179, 187 background, 204, 217

Yuki Sugiura
Page 197

Lucinda Symons
Page 151 inset

Ian Wallace
Page 235

Kate Whitaker
Pages 7 & 8 background, 11, 13 background, 14, 24, 27 & 28 background, 36 background, 45–46, 56, 63 background, 64, 67, 71, 75 background, 79–80, 85 background, 86, 90, 93 background, 97, 107 background, 108, 111–112, 117, 118 background, 126, 129, 133 background, 137, 141 background, 151 background, 155–156, 159, 160 background, 163, 167, 169, 171 background, 172 background, 176 background, 180, 184, 191–192, 196, 199–200, 203 background, 209 background, 210, 213–214, 218 background, 222 background, 225 background, 226, 229, 230 background, 233, 234 background

Isobel Wield
Page 98

Polly Wreford
Page 52